Great Medical Discoveries

Anesthetics

by William W. Lace

LUCENT BOOKS®

THOMSON
™
GALE

San Diego • Detroit • New York • San Francisco • Cleveland • New Haven, Conn. • Waterville, Maine • London • Munich

THOMSON

GALE

© 2004 by Lucent Books. Lucent Books is an imprint of The Gale Group, Inc.,
a division of Thomson Learning, Inc.

Lucent Books® and Thomson Learning™ are trademarks used herein under license.

For more information, contact
Lucent Books
27500 Drake Rd.
Farmington Hills, MI 48331-3535
Or you can visit our Internet site at http://www.gale.com

LIBRARY OF CONGRESS CATALOGING-IN-PUBLICATION DATA

Lace, William W.
    Anesthetics / William W. Lace.
        p. cm. — (Great medical discoveries)
    Includes bibliographical references and index.
    Contents: Knife and pain—First steps, false starts—"No humbug"—Chloroform and the
    spread of anesthesia—New drugs, new deliveries, new deliverers—Mixed blessing.
        ISBN 1-56006-924-4 (hardback : alk. paper)
        1. Anesthetics—Juvenile literature. [1. Anesthetics—History. 2. Anesthetics.] I. Title.
    II. Series.
        RD81.L25 2004
        617.9'6—dc22

Printed in the United States of America

CONTENTS

FOREWORD

Throughout history, people have struggled to understand and conquer the diseases and physical ailments that plague us. Once in a while, a discovery has changed the course of medicine and sometimes, the course of history itself. The stories of these discoveries have many elements in common—accidental findings, sudden insights, human dedication, and most of all, powerful results. Many illnesses that in the past were essentially a death warrant for their sufferers are today curable or even virtually extinct. And exciting new directions in medicine promise a future in which the building blocks of human life itself—the genes—may be manipulated and altered to restore health or to prevent disease from occurring in the first place.

It has been said that an insight is simply a rearrangement of already-known facts, and as often as not, these great medical discoveries have resulted partly from a reexamination of earlier efforts in light of new knowledge. Nineteenth-century monk Gregor Mendel experimented with pea plants for years, quietly unlocking the mysteries of genetics. However, the importance of his findings went unnoticed until three separate scientists, studying cell division with a newly improved invention called a microscope, rediscovered his work decades after his death. French doctor Jean-Antoine Villemin's experiments with rabbits proved that tuberculosis was contagious, but his conclusions were politely ignored by the medical community until another doctor, Robert Koch of Germany, discovered the exact culprit—the tubercle bacillus germ—years later.

Accident, too, has played a part in some medical discoveries. Because the tuberculosis germ does not stain with dye as easily as other bacteria, Koch was able to see it only after he had let a treated slide sit far longer than he intended. An unwanted speck of mold led Englishman Alexander Fleming to recognize the bacteria-killing qualities of the penicillium fungi, ushering in the era of antibiotic "miracle drugs."

That researchers sometimes benefited from fortuitous accidents does not mean that they were bumbling amateurs who relied solely on luck. They were dedicated scientists whose work created the conditions under which such lucky events could occur; many sacrificed years of their lives to observation and experimentation. Sometimes the price they paid was higher. Rene Launnec, who invented the stethoscope to help him study the effects of tuberculosis, himself succumbed to the disease.

And humanity has benefited from these scientists' efforts. The formerly terrifying disease of smallpox has been eliminated from the face of the earth—the only case of the complete conquest of a once deadly disease. Tuberculosis, perhaps the oldest disease known to humans and certainly one of its most prolific killers, has been essentially wiped out in some parts of the world. Genetically engineered insulin is a godsend to countless diabetics who are allergic to the animal insulin that has traditionally been used to help them.

Despite such triumphs there are few unequivocal success stories in the history of great medical discoveries. New strains of tuberculosis are proving to be resistant to the antibiotics originally developed to treat them, raising the specter of a resurgence of the disease that has killed 2 billion people over the course of human history. But medical research continues on numerous fronts and will no doubt lead to still undreamed-of advancements in the future.

Each volume in the Great Medical Discoveries series tells the story of one great medical breakthrough—the first gropings for understanding, the pieces that came together and how, and the immediate and longer-term results. Part science and part social history, the series explains some of the key findings that have shaped modern medicine and relieved untold human suffering. Numerous primary and secondary source quotations enhance the text and bring to life all the drama of scientific discovery. Sidebars highlight personalities and convey personal stories. The series also discusses the future of each medical discovery—a future in which vaccines may guard against AIDS, gene therapy may eliminate cancer, and other as-yet unimagined treatments may become commonplace.

INTRODUCTION

Now and Then

No one enjoys going to a dentist to have a tooth pulled, even though the tooth may be extremely painful. The experience, although still not completely painless, is nevertheless a far cry from what it was prior to 1846. Back then, there was no anesthesia—that is, drugs that eliminate most of the pain associated with surgery and other medical procedures.

Today, a dentist injects a drug—usually a form of procaine, a derivative of cocaine—into the jaw near whichever nerve leads to the afflicted tooth. The patient feels no more than a pinprick.

Within a few minutes, the jaw is completely numb. The dentist then reaches into the patient's mouth with specialized forceps and pulls the tooth. The patient will experience no more than a dull feeling of movement. The only pain associated with the procedure is the injection of the drug.

In more extensive dental procedures, such as surgery on the gums, the anesthesia is slightly different. Most likely, another type of drug—probably a barbiturate—flows into the bloodstream through a tube and a needle that has been inserted into a vein.

Dim Awareness

Unlike a tooth extraction, gum and other oral surgeries can last an hour or more. The patient is semiconscious —only dimly aware of what the dentist is doing—and feels only slight tugs or pulls. Afterward, the patient may not remember the surgery at all.

There is some slight degree of pain—medical professionals prefer the term *discomfort*—with virtually any surgical procedure, dental or otherwise, even with the use of modern anesthetics. Today's patients experience next to nothing, however, compared to what preceded the discovery of anesthesia.

At that time, the pain of dental surgery or any other kind of surgical procedure was something that simply had to be endured. Few people were willing to do so until the pain of the ailment grew greater than their fear of the pain the surgery promised. Worse, in terms of prospects of success, fear of pain caused many people to put off going to a dentist or doctor for so long that their conditions grew far more serious and difficult to treat.

When the pain finally drove one to seek treatment, the procedures were crude. For example, patients would be seated in the dentist's chair with a wooden block inserted between their upper and lower jaws to hold them apart. The dentist would then grasp the diseased tooth with forceps and pull it, often having to

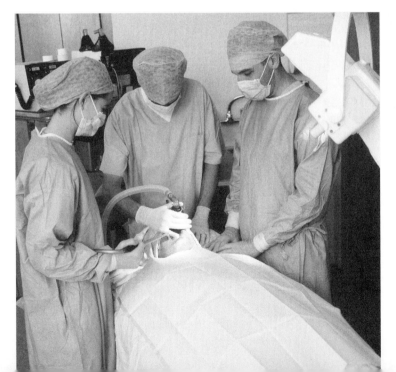

A team of dentists waits for an anesthetic to take effect before treating a patient. Anesthesia is used to dull the pain associated with surgical procedures.

loosen it first by wrenching it back and forth in its socket.

Excruciating Pain

The pain from such procedures was excruciating. Some patients bore it with fortitude—silently and uncomplaining. Others may have fortified themselves with a shot or two of whiskey beforehand. Still others, however, once they had been coaxed into the dentist's chair, had to be held there, either by the dentist's assistants or by the dentist, who would place one knee on the patient's chest.

As painful as minor dental surgery was before anesthesia was discovered, that was trivial compared to what major surgery—such as the removal of a tumor or amputation of an arm or a leg—involved. Prior to the mid-1800s, the operating theater, or room, was a place described by Scottish surgeon John Struthers as "ringing with the groans and shrieks of the patient."[1] The discovery of surgical anesthesia—something that would make a surgical patient completely unconscious or oblivious to pain—would become one of humanity's greatest blessings, making the operating room a place more of healing than of horror.

Prior to the discovery of anesthesia, patients undergoing amputations and other major surgeries endured excruciating pain.

CHAPTER 1

Knife and Pain

Throughout history pain has been one of human-kind's most constant, yet most unwelcome, companions. Almost from the time people learned to record their feelings, pain has been a prominent subject. The agony an ancient Babylonian princess experienced echoes through the ages from the cuneiform writing on the walls of her tomb: "Pain has seized my body. May God tear this pain out."[2] And, as constant and persistent as pain itself have been the efforts of countless doctors to find something—anything—to prevent pain.

Surgery and the pain associated with it are as old, and even older, than civilization. Human remains dating to prehistoric times show evidence of limb amputation and even a primitive form of brain surgery. The Egyptians, Babylonians, and Assyrians left written and pictorial records of surgical operations. As knowledge of human anatomy progressed, more complex surgeries were practiced in India, China, Greece, and Rome.

Pain was an inevitable part of the surgical process, and both the patient and the surgeon were supposed to accept it. The Roman physician Celsus, who lived during the first century A.D., wrote, "Resolved to heal the sufferer entrusted to his care, the surgeon must ignore cries and pleadings, and do his work regardless of complaints."[3]

Most surgeons resolved that operations, if they could not be painless, could at least be short. A skilled surgeon could perform an amputation, start to finish, in five minutes. A lithotomy, an operation to remove bladder stones, could take as little as one minute. Speed not only could save patients from prolonged agony but also could save their lives. Many patients died on the surgical table, not from whatever ailed them or even from loss of blood during the surgery, but because their bodies went into irreversible shock because of the pain.

A Surgeon's Wish

Although surgeons could close their ears to the cries of their patients, most could not close their minds or hearts. Dr. John C. Warren, who would figure prominently in the discovery of anesthesia, once wrote:

> What surgeon is there who has not felt, while witnessing the distress of long painful operations, a sinking of the

An eighteenth-century Persian painting depicts a cesarean section. Before anesthesia, surgeons completed such procedures quickly in order to minimize pain.

heart, to which no habit could render him insensible! What surgeon has not at these times been inspired with a wish, to find some means of lessening the sufferings he was obliged to inflict.[4]

The search for something to relieve pain dates back as far as recorded history and probably well beyond. Ancient peoples, knowing nothing about the causes of pain—except for such obvious ones as wounds or burns—ascribed it to the supernatural. Earliest historical records indicate that people blamed demons, and elaborate rituals were practiced to drive away these evil forces. Natural substances were sometimes used as part of such rituals, and some of these actually were effective in relieving pain. For example, smoke from burning hemp *(Cannabis indica)* seemed to soothe the afflicted person. But, although natural substances might lessen pain, they could not stop it completely unless they were used in amounts considered too dangerous.

Somewhat later, the supernatural view of pain expanded. In addition to demons, gods were thought to afflict people with pain as punishment for wrongdoing. Certainly the Greeks believed this: their word *poine*, meaning "punishment" or "payment," has given us the modern word *pain.*

Christianity and Islam inherited this point of view from Judaism, whose creation story in the book of Genesis 3:16 has God telling Eve that she will bear children "in pain" or "in sorrow" because of having eaten the forbidden fruit in the Garden of Eden. As a result of such ideas, efforts at pain relief were a mixture of magic and medicine for thousands of years.

Mandrake

Whatever people might have believed about the cause for pain, they clearly sought ways to alleviate it. One of the most effective, at least as described in ancient writings, was mandragora or mandrake, an excellent example of how tightly medicine and magic were intertwined.

Before Anesthesia

Anesthesia—the elimination or diminution of pain—has come to be such an accepted part of surgery that it is difficult to imagine what patients must have suffered before its discovery. In fact, today's patients do not have to use their imaginations since several firsthand accounts survive. This account of a treatment for a dislocated hip was written during the mid-1800s by eyewitness Nathan Rice. It is found in Victory over Pain *by Betty MacQuitty.*

A pulley is attached to the affected limb, while the body, trussed up by appropriate bands, is fastened to another; now several powerful muscular assistants seize the ropes, and with a careful, steady drawing, tighten the cords. Soon the tension makes itself felt, and as the stubborn muscles stretch and yield to the strain, one can almost imagine that he hears the crack of parting sinews. Big drops of perspiration, started by the excess of agony, bestrew the patient's forehead, sharp screams burst forth from him in peal after peal—all his struggles to free himself and escape the horrid torture are valueless, for he is in the powerful hands of men then as inexorable as death. . . . Stronger comes the pull, more force is added to the ropes, the tugs, cruel and unyielding, seem as if they would burst the tendons where they stand out like whipcords. At last the agony becomes too great for human endurance, and with a wild, despairing yell, the suffering patient relapses into unconsciousness. . . . The surgeon avails himself of the opportunity and . . . seizing the limb, by a dexterous twist snaps the head of the bone into its socket. The operation is done, and the poor prostrated, bruised sufferer can be removed to his pallet to recover from the fearful results of the operation as best he can.

The mandrake plant was supposedly so powerful that it could only be safely uprooted by moonlight, not by hand, but by a cord attached to a black dog. The thick, forked root of the mandrake was supposed to somewhat resemble the human body, and according to legend, its shriek when pulled from the ground could drive a person insane.

In addition to providing a pain-free sleep, the mandrake could supposedly heal disease, induce love, and facilitate pregnancy. Its properties were described and praised by such writers as the Greek poet Homer around 650 B.C., the Jewish historian Josephus in about A.D. 100, and the Greek physician Galen in about A.D. 200. References to mandrake can be found as late as the mid-1600s, but there is no hard evidence that such

The Mandrake Ritual

Although its existence has never been documented, the mandrake plant was supposed to have powerful abilities to prevent pain. Those who would use it, though, had to be very careful about how it was gathered, as this passage by Andrew Lang, found in The Evolution of Anesthesia *by M.H. Armstrong Davison, shows.*

He who desires to possess a mandrake must stop his ears with wax, so that he may not hear the deadly yells which the plant utters as it is being dragged from the earth. Then, before sunrise on a Friday, the amateur goes out with a dog, "all black," makes three crosses round the mandrake, loosens the soil about the root, ties the root to the dog's tail and offers the beast a piece of bread. The dog runs at the bread, drags out the mandrake root, and falls dead, killed by the horrible yell of the plant.

A fifteenth-century medical illustration of the mandrake plant, once reputed to have anesthetic properties.

a plant ever really existed. There is a plant, *Atropina mandragora*, a member of the belladonna, or deadly nightshade, family, but it was not given that name until the mid-1700s, and it has none of the supposed attributes of the mandrake.

Other naturally anesthetic drugs were unquestionably real, and they—or substances derived from them—are still in use. For example, the Indian hemp plant is the source of both marijuana, made from the leaves, and hashish, made from the flowers. While both drugs have been used principally to produce an altered mental state, some ancient physicians had patients inhale the fumes until they became unconscious.

Opium

Much more powerful than the drugs derived from hemp was opium, a product of the poppy flower (*Papaver somniferum*). Doctors extracted opium from the unripe seeds of the flower and mixed it with a drink, usually wine, to produce unconsciousness. Other extracts, such as those from hemlock and henbane, were used in a similar manner.

Another favorite way of administering painkilling drugs was by placing them in a liquid mixture, using the mixture to soak a sponge, and holding the sponge under the patient's nostrils. The Italian physician Nicolas of Salerno, who lived during the 1100s, left a recipe for what he called a *spongia somnifera*, or sleep-producing sponge. In it were "opium thebaicum, juice of hyoscyamine, unripened berry of the blackberry, lettuce seed, juice of hemlock, poppy, mandragora, ivy."[5]

No matter how it was administered, for many centuries opium was the principal drug relied on by doctors to relieve pain, but it was normally used in a diluted form. Laudanum, for instance, was a solution of opium in an alcohol base and was widely used in Europe as a sedative until the 1800s. Another opium mixture, paregoric, was used to treat diarrhea and intestinal pain.

The seeds of the poppy flower have long been used for their sedative and painkilling properties.

PAPAVER SOMNIFERUM L.
Der Schlafmachende Mohn.

Despite their obvious power, the use of opium, hemlock, henbane, and other drugs for general anesthesia—to render a person totally unconscious before surgery—was never widespread. At high doses, the drugs were too dangerous and their effects on individual patients unpredictable. Chemists could distill them from their natural sources, but there was no way to be assured of the strength of the products. Moreover, different patients required different amounts of the drug depending on body weight and other factors. Patients who were drugged into unconsciousness too often slipped from unconsciousness into death.

In this sixteenth-century painting, a Dominican monk inhales alcohol fumes to deaden the pain as his lay brothers burn stigmata on his hands and feet.

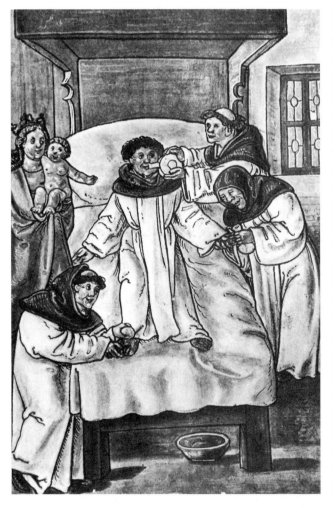

Pain or Punishment?

So it was that most doctors chose to let their surgical patients suffer terrible pain rather than risk the consequences of using opium or other drugs. Indeed, those who engaged in such practices were shunned by their colleagues. During the 1600s a man named Bailly in the French city of Troyes used drugs to put a patient to sleep. Gui Patin of the University of Paris medical faculty protested: "Herbal poisons have worked mischief in more skillful hands than his. See to it that these practices are not allowed, and do not let him go unpunished."[6] Bailly was fined, and the drugging of patients before operations was forbidden by law.

A commonly used and far less dangerous substance used to alleviate the pain of surgery was alcohol. Patients undergoing minor dental surgery might imbibe rum or whiskey beforehand, as much to calm their nerves as to stop pain. On battlefields or warships, surgeons would allow a wounded man to drink as much as he was able, then operate as quickly as possible once the patient was intoxicated.

Alcohol as an anesthetic, however, did pose some dangers. Patients could drink themselves into complete insensibility, but in so doing they ran the risk of alcohol poisoning and death. And any lesser quantity of alcohol might dull pain but would not eliminate it.

Physical Means

Some people tried to find ways of eliminating pain without resorting to drugs of any kind. Some attempts were purely physical, with no use of outside agents. For example, physicians in ancient Assyria ligated, or bound, a limb to be operated on, placing pressure on blood vessels and nerves. In colder climates, the target area might be placed in frigid water or packed in ice to render it numb.

Still others thought that no physical means of any kind were required. Pain, they maintained, was a manifestation of the mind and could be controlled. The Stoic philosophers of ancient Greece and Rome taught that pain could be overcome by the power of an individual's mind without dependence on religious faith or intervention by gods or saints. The Stoics held that all people had within themselves the power to banish pain by "rational repudiation." That is, one could simply eliminate pain through strength of will, denying its existence.

For some, however, conquering pain was a matter of religious faith. For example, Muhammad, the founder of Islam, instructed his followers who suffered from toothaches to put one of their fingers on the sore spot and recite from the Koran.

Mesmerism

The idea that some sort of external force could free the body from pain and disease found great popularity in the work of the German physician Franz Mesmer, who earned his medical degree in 1766. According to Mesmer, cosmic energies exist that, if properly harnessed and directed, can eliminate pain. He said that some people, including himself, were capable of channeling such energies to others and curing disease.

Practicing in France, Mesmer first used magnets, attaching them to his patients' bodies. Many patients pronounced themselves improved. Eventually, so that he could treat more people at once, Mesmer claimed to have transferred his "animal magnetism" into a stick with which he could cure people by touching them or merely pointing at them.

In 1874 Mesmer was found to be a fraud by a French commission. Part of his procedures, however, had included putting people into trances, and those subjected to such treatments were said to have been "mesmerized." A follower of Mesmer, Maxime de Puységur, found that he was able to put people in trances so deep they could not feel pain.

Oddly, patients in these deep trances could—and did—still move about. For this reason de Puységur called his method somnambulism, or sleepwalking, and it was later renamed hypnosis. In the early 1800s it was used by doctors throughout Europe as a way to treat persons suffering from pain. Soon, surgeons wondered if somnambulism could provide unconsciousness safer than that induced by drugs.

Scorned by Colleagues

The two principal proponents of somnambulistic surgery were doctors John Elliotson and James Esdaile, both of Scotland. Their theories, however, aroused the scorn of the medical establishment, which considered somnambulism something practiced only by quacks and charlatans on unsuspecting patients.

Elliotson was forced to resign from University Hospital in Edinburgh, but Esdaile took his procedure to India, and there he had such success that a hospital was provided for him. He reported having performed pain-free procedures from surface tumors to arm and leg amputations. The reports were so numerous and positive that doctors in Europe and the United States—including Dr. John Warren in Boston—tried to achieve similar results. None succeeded in doing so, and Warren and others returned to subjecting their patients to the horrors afforded by the operating rooms of the time.

Franz Mesmer claimed he could cure patients by putting them in deep trances, a procedure first known as somnambulism and later renamed hypnosis.

Before anesthesia, surgeons did their work mostly in the most remote parts of a hospital—high in an attic or deep in a basement—so that the screams of sufferers would not disturb their fellow patients. According to one eyewitness of a preanesthesia operation, a patient's determination to remain calm and still, no matter how severe the pain, would vanish at the first touch of the scalpel:

> But of what avail are all her attempts at fortitude? At the first clear crisp cut of the scalpel, agonising screams burst from her and with convulsive struggles she endeavours to leap from the table. But the force is nigh. Strong men throw themselves upon her and pinion her limbs. Shrieks upon shrieks make their horrible way into the stillness of the room, until the heart of the boldest sinks in his bosom like a lump of lead.[7]

Surgery Under Mesmerism

One of the leading advocates of mesmerism, a form of hypnotism to relieve pain during surgery, was John Elliotson, a professor in Scotland. His description of an operation performed under mesmerism is found in Triumph over Pain: The Story of Anesthesia *by Robert H. Curtis. Elliotson quotes the mesmerist, a Mr. Topham, as saying:*

Mr. Ward [the surgeon], after one earnest look at the man, slowly plunged his knife into the centre of the outside of the thigh, directly to the bone, and then made a clear incision round the bone, to the opposite point on the inside of the thigh. The stillness at this moment was something awful; the calm respiration of the sleeping man alone was heard, for all other sound seemed suspended.

For his part, the surgeon reported:

The placid look of countenance never changed for an instant; his whole frame rested, in perfect stillness and repose, not a muscle was seen to twitch. To the end of the operation, including the sawing of the bone, securing the arteries, and applying the bandages, occupying a period of upwards of twenty minutes, he lay like a statue.

Events that had been unfolding for centuries, however, were about to culminate in a discovery that would make such scenes things of the past. It was not a sudden discovery, a scientific breakthrough as the result of a bold experiment. Rather, it was the falling into place of puzzle pieces that had been around for many years. The tragedy was that so many people had to endure such suffering before the pieces were finally put together.

CHAPTER 2

First Steps, False Starts

Perhaps rather than a puzzle, the discovery of anesthesia can be compared to a road leading up a steep hill. Following scientific signposts along the way, investigators repeatedly seemed poised to reach the summit only to turn aside just short of their goal out of concerns about the safety of the substances they were studying. The substances—nitrous oxide, ether, and morphine—would eventually become effective anesthetics, but, ironically, they were first used for recreation. As a result, humanity had to wait half a century or more for blessings of anesthesia.

Ether, the anesthetic that would at long last gain the attention of the medical community and then the world, was discovered some six hundred years beforehand. Scientist and philosopher Ramon Llull, working sometime in the 1200s, combined alcohol with sulfuric acid, thereby producing a white fluid. Since the new substance had a strong, sickly sweet smell and since the common name for sulfuric acid was vitriol, Llull named it sweet vitriol.

Little was heard of sweet vitriol for about two hundred years. Then, in the 1400s, a Swiss doctor with the unlikely name of Philippus Aureolus Theophrastus Bombast von Hohenheim made it the subject of one of his countless experiments.

Bombast von Hohenheim, better known as Paracelsus, a name he adopted since he considered himself superior to the famous Roman physician Celsus, induced various animals, including chickens, to drink sweet vitriol—with remarkable results. He wrote that the substance

> has an agreeable taste, so that even chickens take it gladly, and thereafter fall asleep for a long time, awaking undamaged. In view of the effects of this vitriol, I think it especially noteworthy that its use may be recommended for painful illnesses, and that it will mitigate the disagreeable complications of these.[8]

Paracelsus was an eccentric character who rejected formal education, even though he earned his medical degree at the age of fifteen, and who preferred to wander Europe investigating folk remedies. It was little

In a series of experiments with farm animals, the Swiss doctor Paracelsus observed the soporific effects of sweet vitriol, or ether, a concoction of alcohol and sulfuric acid.

wonder, then, that his observations were ignored by the leading doctors of his day.

Paracelsus's Notes

One of Paracelsus's disciples, Valerius Cordus, compiled an exhaustive list of his master's many concoctions, complete with their characteristics and directions for their preparation and use. In 1542, a year after Paracelsus died, Cordus showed his list to doctors in the German city of Nuremberg. They were impressed, and the city agreed to buy his collection of notes.

For reasons historians have not been able to identify, the voluminous notes were put aside and eventually forgotten. There were scattered references to sweet vitriol over the next one hundred years, including those in works by such noted scientists as physicist Isaac Newton and chemist Robert Boyle, but there is no evidence that anyone followed up on Paracelsus's experiments.

Scientists did not resume trying to discover a use for sweet vitriol until the 1700s. One of them gave it the name ether, after the substance believed by many at the time to fill all space above the sphere of the moon and to compose the stars and planets. The first reference to ether as a medicine came in 1743, and in 1795 one English doctor wrote that, when inhaled, it "abates the hectic heat, relieves and often removes the dyspnoea [difficult breathing], and promotes and often improves the expectoration [removal of mucus from the throat and lungs]."[9]

Michael Faraday, who would be better known for his work with electricity, discovered the anesthetic effect of ether during early 1800s while working as an assistant to chemist Humphry Davy, who was conducting experiments with nitrous oxide, or laughing gas. In an 1818 journal Faraday wrote:

> When the vapour of ether is mixed with common air and inhaled, it produces effects very similar to those of nitrous oxide. By the incautious breathing of ether vapour a man

was thrown into a lethargic condition which, with few interruptions, lasted for thirty hours.[10]

Faraday, however, was merely an assistant, nitrous oxide was the principal subject of the article, and the reference to ether was buried deep within the text. No one followed up on it, and for his part, Faraday moved on to other fields.

Ether Frolics

Ether, meanwhile, became a plaything. One of the similarities between ether and nitrous oxide, noted by Faraday, was their intoxicating effect. During the first half of the 1800s, "ether frolics" were popular, especially in the United States, among young men and women. A small amount of ether, mixed with hot water in an air-tight bladder, produced vapors that, when breathed through a tube, caused participants to act foolishly as if drunk with alcohol. Occasionally, someone would breathe too much and become unconscious, but no one seemed to take any special note of this.

Most prominent doctors thought ether was of little use. One professor wrote in an 1825 textbook that "its impressions are so evanescent [transient] that little is gained by it, and it is difficult to imagine a case in which it should supersede wine." In the same book, coming tantalizingly close to the great discovery, he quotes an article advancing the idea that "ether acts directly as a sedative on the spinal system."[11] Neither he nor anyone else followed this clue, and the discovery had to wait.

The substance that held the most interest for Davy and Faraday was nitrous oxide, discovered by British chemist Joseph Priestley in 1772. Priestley created the gas by treating iron filings with nitric acid, but no one attempted to find a use for it until 1799, when Dr. Thomas Beddoes began to use various gases to treat diseases.

Heretofore, medicinal substances had been either applied directly to the skin or given internally. Priestley had the notion that some gases might be beneficial if inhaled directly, and Beddoes picked up on his idea, opening a clinic, the Pneumatic Institute, in the city of Bristol. His goal was to apply "the different types of air"[12] to help relieve respiratory illnesses.

To direct his institute Beddoes chose Humphry Davy, at this time a twenty-one-year-old apprentice to a surgeon in a nearby city. Davy's passion was chemistry, and much of his experimentation, done privately on his own time when his duties as an apprentice were finished, had been with nitrous oxide.

Michael Faraday, who later became famous for his work with electricity, discovered the anesthetic effect of ether during the early 1800s.

Self-Experimentation

Even though Priestley and others held that nitrous oxide was poisonous and breathing it could be fatal, Davy decided to try some on himself. Such self-experimentation was not uncommon in the 1800s, long before the time when drugs would be subjected to carefully controlled clinical trials before being tried on humans. Davy was more reckless than most. A friend wrote, "He seemed to act as if, in case of sacrificing one life, he had two or three others in reserve on which he could fall back in case of necessity."[13]

When Davy inhaled nitrous oxide fumes, he first felt a sense of lightness and relaxation, soon followed by an uncontrollable urge to laugh. Soon, if Davy's employer needed him at night, he might find his

apprentice laughing helplessly on the floor of his room. It was no wonder that Davy gave nitrous oxide the new name of laughing gas.

Eventually, the surgeon agreed to try laughing gas himself. He was amazed at the result and even more amazed when Davy told him that he had noticed that the gas tended to relieve pain, as when he had been suffering from inflamed gums. The surgeon urged Davy to continue his experiments, hoping to put the gas to use with his patients.

Shortly afterward, Davy moved to Beddoes's Pneumatic Institute. Soon, he was experimenting not only on himself but also on some of Bristol's most socially prominent citizens, including poets Samuel

Taylor Coleridge and William Wordsworth. He and Beddoes began using nitrous oxide to treat people with asthma, and their patients reported themselves greatly improved. Increasingly, however, Davy was intrigued with laughing gas, not as a therapy but as a painkiller.

Findings Are Published

Davy found that the gas dulled pain in his patients in addition to producing exhilaration. He succeeded in curing his own headaches by breathing the vapors. Finally, in 1800 he published a book, *Researches, Chemical and Philosophical; Chiefly Concerning Nitrous Oxide.* In it, Davy writes, "Since nitrous oxide seems capable of destroying physical pain, it may be used in surgical operations where there is not great effusion of blood."[14]

In other words, Davy said, laughing gas could perhaps dull the pain of a minor operation. Although he

The Thrill of Laughing Gas

On April 12, 1799, English chemist Humphry Davy, who recently had succeeded in making pure nitrous oxide, later called laughing gas, tried it out on himself. After recovering from the effects of the gas, he wrote this description of his experience, found in Triumph over Pain *by René Fülöp-Miller.*

A thrilling extending from the chest to the extremities was almost immediately produced. I felt a sense of tangible extension highly pleasurable in every limb; my visible impressions were dazzling, and apparently magnified, I heard distinctly every sound in the room, and was perfectly aware of my situation. By degrees, as the pleasurable sensations increased, I lost all connection with external things; trains of visible images rapidly passed through my mind, and were connected with words in such a manner, as to produce perceptions perfectly novel. I existed in a world of newly connected and newly modified ideas: I theorized, I imagined that I made discoveries. . . . As I recovered my former state of mind I felt an inclination to communicate the discoveries I had made during the experiment. I endeavoured to recall the ideas: they were feeble and indistinct; one collection of terms however presented itself; and with a most intense belief and prophetic manner, I exclaimed . . . "Nothing exists but thoughts! The universe is composed of impressions, ideas, pleasures, and pains."

had observed that large doses could sometimes make a person unconscious—and, indeed, he had occasionally made himself unconscious—he failed to see that nitrous oxide also might permit pain-free major surgeries.

Davy might have gone on to make this discovery, but laughing gas was getting a bad name. Doctors had found that it could result in a dangerously slow heartbeat in some users. Treatment by gas inhalation became less popular, its practitioners were denounced by the medical establishment, and laughing gas inhalation was finally made illegal in Great Britain. Beddoes had to convert his clinic into a conventional hospital, and Davy moved on to other scientific pursuits.

Davy's work was taken up in the 1820s by Henry Hill Hickman, a doctor in the English city of Ludlow. Experimenting on animals, he developed a procedure for relaxing his subject with carbon dioxide vapor, then administering nitrous oxide to bring about unconsciousness.

In 1824 Hickman sought permission to try his method on human subjects. No one seemed interested, not even Davy or Faraday. Hickman read a paper on his experiments before the Medical Society of London and was called a dreamer and a fool. He tried his luck in France, appealing to King Charles X in 1828. The king recommended that the French Academy of Medicine investigate, but it did nothing. Hickman returned to England and died there two years later, only twenty-nine years old. Nitrous oxide, in the meantime, went the way of ether—a source of popular amusement.

Morphine

The stories of ether and nitrous oxide were to be repeated with morphine. The pain-relieving properties of opium, from which morphine would be derived, had been known for centuries, but doctors avoided using it because of the dangers involved. The dose that might be too small in one patient would kill another.

The Popular View

The use of nitrous oxide, or laughing gas, as a source of amusement was widespread in both Europe and the United States in the early 1800s. One frequent and enthusiastic user was Thomas Green Fessenden, a New Hampshire native living in London. Fessenden was so taken with laughing gas that he wrote a poem about it, this excerpt of which is found in Ether Day *by Julie M. Fenster.*

What then occurs? A lucky hit—
I've found a substitute for wit.
Beddoes (bless the good doctor) has
Sent me a bag full of his gas
Which snuffed the nose up, makes wit brighter,
And ekes [makes larger] a dunce an airy writer.

How swiftly this giddy world round,
Like tortur'd top, by truant twirl'd round;
I'm larger grown from head to tail
Than mammoth, elephant or whale!—
Now feel a "tangible extension"
Of semi-infinite dimension!—

Inflated with supreme intensity,
I fill three quarters of immensity!
But now, alas! A wicked wag
Has pull'd away the gaseous bag:
From heaven, where thron'd like Jove I sat,
I'm fall'n! fall'n! down, flat! flat! flat!

Nitrous oxide became a popular source of entertainment throughout the United States and Europe in the early 1800s.

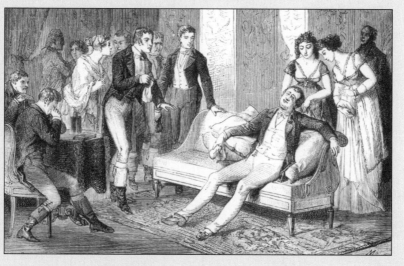

The man who solved the problem, like Davy and Faraday before him, did much of his work while still an apprentice. Friederich Sertürner lived in the German town of Paderborn, working for a pharmacist. His master, along with most doctors, was reconciled to the fact that opium was too dangerous to use.

Sertürner, however, was curious. Everyone knew that the poppy produced opium, but what was it in the seeds that gave opium its characteristics? Sertürner set out to find what later scientists would call the active principle—the specific chemical within a natural substance that produces particular effects. If this substance could be isolated, Sertürner reasoned, exact doses could be measured out.

In 1803 he began to experiment by treating raw opium with a variety of solvents. One, liquid ammonia, caused white crystals to form. After Sertürner cleansed the crystals to remove any impurities, he tested them on mice and dogs. Not only did this new substance dull pain, but it produced unconsciousness. As with opium, too large a dose caused death, but Sertürner thought that, through experimentation, the correct doses could be determined.

Sertürner tested the drug on himself and some friends, carefully noting the effects. A meticulous researcher, he published his findings in an obscure paper in 1806, but it was not until 1817, once he was an established pharmacist, that he submitted a major article to a medical journal. Sertürner called his discovery morphium, after the Greek god of dreams; later on, the name was changed to morphine.

Sertürner gained wide recognition for his discovery. Seven universities awarded him doctorate degrees. The prestigious Institute of France awarded him a prize as a "Benefactor of Humanity." So much attention aroused the jealously of colleagues, who resented the success of someone they considered a self-trained upstart. They belittled his discovery, claiming that morphine still was too dangerous. Embittered, Sertürner turned away from his work with morphine and pursued other ideas, including more efficient guns and new kinds of gunpowder.

Crawford Long

Faraday, Davy, Hickman, and Sertürner stopped just short of the summit of the road to anesthesia. Another man, Dr. Crawford Long, actually reached the summit in 1842 but failed to let anyone know.

Ether frolics were a common source of amusement in rural Georgia, where Long had his medical practice. Indeed, Long provided the ether for many such parties himself. He noticed, as had Davy with nitrous oxide, that ether seemed to prevent pain as well as produce intoxication. "I would frequently . . . discover bruised or painful spots on my person which I had no recollection of causing," he later wrote. "I notice my friends while etherized received falls or blows which I believed were sufficient to produce pain."[15]

Like others before him, Long wondered if ether could be used to prevent pain in surgery. Unlike those others, however, he put his curiosity to the test. One of his patients, James V. Venable, had postponed the removal of two neck tumors twice, fearing the pain. Long persuaded him that the operation might be done painlessly with ether. Venable agreed, and on March 30 Long placed a towel soaked in ether over his patient's face. Venable swiftly became unconscious, and Long removed the tumors.

In 1842 Crawford Long became the first physician to perform a surgical procedure on a patient anesthetized with ether.

Crawford Long's Operation

The first physician to perform surgery under what is known now as anesthesia was Crawford Long of Jefferson, Georgia. Long made no attempt, however, to share his discovery. Only in 1849, when a controversy had broken out about who discovered anesthesia and when, did Long write about his 1842 operation on James V. Venable. This excerpt is found in The First Anesthetic *by Frank Kells Boland.*

The ether was given to Mr. Venable on a towel; and when fully under its influence I extirpated the tumour. It was encysted, and about half an inch in diameter. The patient continued to inhale ether during the time of the operation; and when informed it was over, seemed incredulous, until the tumour was shown him. He gave no evidence of suffering during the operation, and assured me, after it was over, that he did not experience the slightest degree of pain from its performance.

Venable added in a notarized statement:

I commenced inhaling the ether before the operation was commenced, and continued it until the operation was over. I did not feel the slightest pain from the operation and could not believe the tumour was removed until it was shown to me.

A month or two after this time, Dr. C.W. Long cut out the other tumour, situated on the same side of my neck. In this operation I did not feel the least pain until the last cut was made, when I felt a little pain. In this operation, I stopped inhaling the ether before the operation was finished. I inhaled the ether, in both cases, from a towel, which was the common method of taking it.

A Cruel Experiment

Later, Long was called on to amputate two fingers on the hand of a young slave. In an experiment that would shock people in modern times because of its disregard for another human being, Long used ether before the removal of only one finger. He then waited until the anesthetic had worn off before amputating the second. The patient felt such pain at the second amputation that he had to be tied down.

Long thought he needed to perform more operations on patients under ether before publishing his results. However, he never got the chance. Word of his experiments had gotten around, and local people began whispering that he would probably kill someone before he was through. His medical practice began to decline, and to save it, Long abandoned his work with ether and made no report.

And so, despite several promising attempts, anesthesia had yet to make its impact on medicine. Most surgeons agreed with their French colleague Alfred Velpeau, who in 1839 had said, "To escape pain in surgical operations is a chimera [illusion] which we are not permitted to look for in our day."[16] Little did he realize that the chimera would become a reality within seven years.

CHAPTER 3

"No Humbug"

As the first half of the 1800s was drawing to a close, the conquest of pain seemed no closer than it had been a century earlier when English anatomist John Hunter sniffed that the surgeon was little more than "a savage armed with a knife."[17] All the false starts of the past, however, were about to culminate in a demonstration on October 16, 1846, that would change the world of medicine forever.

The demonstration was the final link in a chain of events that began two years earlier, when Dr. Horace Wells, a dentist in Hartford, Connecticut, attended a laughing gas exhibition—one of the public spectacles to which anesthesia had been relegated. A friend, Sam Cooley, while cavorting about the stage after inhaling the gas, ran hard into a wooden bench, apparently not realizing it.

When Cooley returned to his seat, Wells noticed blood on his friend's trousers. Only when Cooley lifted his trouser leg and saw a deep gash did he feel any pain.

Wells had read Humphry Davy's work and was aware of the properties of nitrous oxide. After the performance, Wells asked Gardner Q. Colton, who had staged the show, "Why cannot a man have a tooth pulled while under the gas and not feel it?"[18] Colton said he did not know, and Wells resolved to find out.

The next morning, Colton brought a bag of nitrous oxide to Wells's office. They called in another dentist, Dr. John Riggs, to pull one of Wells's teeth, which had been giving him some pain. Colton administered the gas. Wells inhaled it deeply and soon slumped in his chair. Riggs quickly applied his forceps and yanked the tooth free. Wells did not stir until a few minutes later. He felt the hole where the tooth had been and said in wonder, "I didn't feel it so much as the prick of a pin!"[19]

Word Spreads

Word of the experiment spread and soon Wells's Hartford office was overrun with patients eager to experience this new marvel. He shared his technique with other dentists in the city. Unlike Crawford Long,

"The Greatest Discovery Ever Made"

On December 11, 1844, a dentist in Hartford, Connecticut, Horace Wells, first used nitrous oxide in a surgical operation. The patient was none other than Wells himself. Gardner Q. Colton, who had exhibited the effects of the gas at a public show the night before, was present and later told what happened. This excerpt is found in Triumph over Pain: The Story of Anesthesia *by Robert H. Curtis.*

I took a bag of gas to his [Wells's] office—Dr. Riggs having been called in—and administered it to Wells and Dr. Riggs extracted a molar tooth from him. Dr. Wells, on recovering, exclaimed, "It is the greatest discovery ever made! I didn't feel it so much as the prick of a pin!" This was the FIRST operation performed in modern anesthesia, and was the forerunning of all other anesthetics. Beyond all question, this discovery had its birth in the brain of Dr. Horace Wells! I can only claim for myself that I was the occasion of the discovery, and having given the gas for the first operation with an anesthetic.

Dentist Horace Wells had himself sedated with nitrous oxide while a colleague extracted one of his teeth in the first surgical procedure using an anesthetic.

however, Wells was determined that the entire world should know of his discovery. What he needed was a demonstration that was both highly visible and medically credible.

Wells chose as the venue for his demonstration the Massachusetts General Hospital in Boston, the most prestigious teaching hospital in the country. He had briefly practiced in Boston in partnership with William T.G. Morton, and it was to Morton he turned for help in arranging a demonstration at the hospital.

Morton was also a dentist, having learned his skills from Wells. When Wells came to see him in Boston in January 1845, Morton took him to see Dr. Charles Jackson, a prominent chemist and geologist whose opinion on scientific matters was highly respected in Boston. Morton had taken a class at Harvard College from Jackson, but when Wells explained his idea, Jackson, as Wells recalled later, "particularly seemed inclined to ridicule the whole thing."[20]

Morton did, however, secure for Wells a meeting with Dr. John Warren, head of surgery at Massachusetts General. Unlike Jackson, Warren was so impressed with Wells's description of nitrous oxide anesthesia that he invited him to lecture to a class of medical students and to perform a demonstration.

On the day that the operation—a leg amputation—was to be performed, however, the patient backed out. One of the medical students volunteered to take his place and have a tooth pulled. Something went wrong. Perhaps the gas that Wells had obtained was not pure, for when he began to pull the tooth, witnesses later recalled, "The patient halloed somewhat."[21] The students shouted that Wells was a humbug and booed him out of the room. He retreated to Hartford in disgrace.

Morton's Experiments

Morton, however, saw possibilities of fame, to say nothing of profit, in anesthesia. He experimented with nitrous oxide in 1845, getting information from an

Chemist Charles Jackson lies unconscious after inhaling ether. Physicians studying the anesthetic effects of various substances often experimented on themselves.

unsuspecting Wells, but later turned his attention to ether. Exactly when and why he changed his focus remains unclear. For his part, Morton said that Jackson had told him in 1844 that ether applied to skin could relieve pain and that he had heard from an assistant about ether frolics.

Morton visited Jackson in September, supposedly to borrow a gas bag for use with nitrous oxide but really to learn what he could about ether. Morton said later he pretended ignorance of ether in order to prevent Jackson from suspecting how close he was to a discovery. Jackson, who gave Morton a complete description of ether's manufacture and effects, later said that it was evident to him that Morton knew nothing about sulfuric ether and must have been experimenting with another kind of ether if, indeed, he had been experimenting at all.

That night, Morton put to use what he had learned from Jackson. He invited a newspaper reporter to be present when he pulled a tooth after administering ether to a patient. The reporter was led to believe that the patient, Eben Frost, had merely happened along, actually, he was a friend of Morton's whose visit had been planned.

At any rate, the tooth was pulled painlessly, and the reporter duly wrote the article, in which he said that the patient "was put into a kind of sleep, by inhaling a preparation."[22] Morton had not told the reporter what the "preparation" was. He hoped to be able to profit by keeping it a secret.

Attracting Attention

Three days later Morton was advertising painless dentistry in Boston newspapers. The advertisements attracted hordes of patients and also the attention of Dr. Henry Bigelow, a junior staff member at Massachusetts

William Morton prepares to administer ether to his patient, Eben Frost, before extracting a tooth.

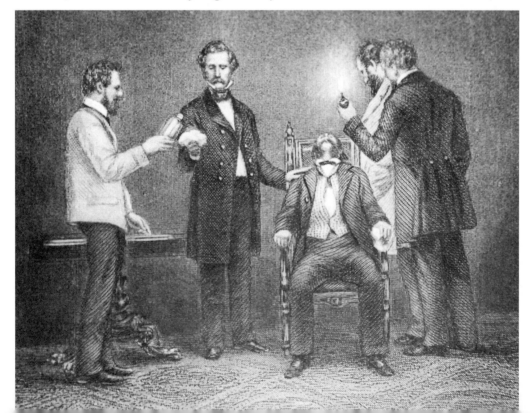

General. Bigelow came to observe Morton at work and was so impressed that he began bringing his colleagues. He then suggested to Morton that he ask Dr. Warren for permission to give a demonstration at the hospital.

It would have been easy for Warren, particularly after the Horace Wells fiasco, to refuse. Warren, however, was not one of those surgeons who unquestioningly accepted pain as part of his calling. He longed for something to relieve his patients' pain and was willing to risk another failure. On October 14 Morton received a letter inviting him to come to Massachusetts General at 10 A.M. on October 16 to perform an operation using his new procedure.

The invitation threw Morton into something of a panic. He was eager to give a demonstration before the leading physicians of Boston, and in one of the nation's most famous hospitals, but he also wanted to make sure he profited. Morton had already taken some steps to this end. On October 1, the morning after his demonstration to a reporter, Morton had consulted an attorney, R.H. Eddy, to explore obtaining a patent on ether. This was entirely counter to the medical ethics of the day. Discoveries were supposed to be shared with the world for the benefit of all humanity, not exploited for profit. In fact, only unscrupulous quacks took out patents on their remedies, thus the derogatory meaning attached to the term *patent medicine*.

Enormous Stakes

The stakes, however, were enormous. Morton and Eddy calculated that a patent on ether anesthesia could bring in, over the fourteen-year life of the patent, a sum equal to about $7 million in today's terms.

Sulfuric ether, however, was a commonly available chemical substance and therefore not eligible for a patent. Although Morton had, indeed, made a great discovery, he had not actually invented anything. He needed something besides common sulfuric ether before he could claim exclusive rights to its use as an anesthetic. Morton solved that problem by adding oil of orange, which had no effect on the ether except to improve its smell.

At the same time, Morton also wanted to take out a patent on the device used to administer the ether. At first he had used nothing more than a handkerchief soaked with ether and placed over the patient's nose and mouth. He soon enhanced his apparatus to include a glass sphere, or retort, which held a sponge soaked in ether. The sphere had a glass tube through which the patient breathed the fumes. It was better than a handkerchief, but still not intricate enough to qualify as an invention in the opinion of the U.S. Patent Office.

On the morning of October 15 Morton rushed to the workshop of Joseph Wightman, a maker of medical instruments. Morton told Wightman of the operation scheduled for the next day and convinced him to put aside whatever he was working on and make improvements in the ether device. Wightman replaced the glass stopper in the tube with a cork through which a much smaller tube could be inserted to replenish the ether. He also cut grooves in the cork to admit air into the sphere, necessary since the patient had to breathe a combination of air and ether fumes to avoid asphyxiation.

More Work Is Needed

Morton was still not satisfied. That night he took the device to his landlord, who happened to be Dr. Augustus Gould, a well-known scientist. Gould suggested a system of valves that would enable air to mix with ether fumes when inhaled but that would prevent air from being exhaled into the sphere.

Just after dawn on October 16, Morton rushed to another instrument maker named Chamberlain, presumably not wishing to impose on Wightman again. Chamberlain studied Morton's drawings and, as

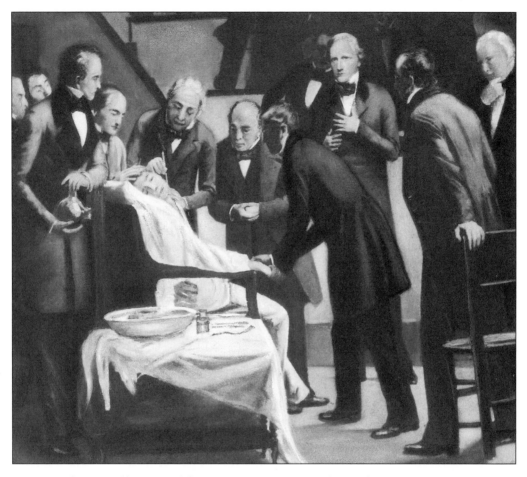

Morton frantically urged him to greater speed, made the changes.

Meanwhile, all was ready at the hospital. The patient, Gilbert Abbot, had a tumor on the left side of his neck, just below the jaw. Abbot was seated in a chair, with the surgical instruments laid out nearby. In front of the chair, rows of seats rose in an amphitheater. They were filled with medical students and curious doctors.

Warren was there, ready to perform the surgery. Gould was there, as was Bigelow, the man who had suggested the demonstration to begin with. Even Eben Frost was there. Just about everyone was there except Morton. Ten o'clock came and went. Warren agreed to wait a while, but at 10:25 he finally said to

John Warren excises a tumor from the neck of Gilbert Abbot in the first surgical procedure to use William Morton's ether apparatus.

the audience sarcastically, "It appears he [Morton] is otherwise engaged."[23] Warren picked up a scalpel, but just as he was about to make the first incision, Morton burst through the door.

"Well, sir," Warren said, "your patient is ready." Morton quickly set up his apparatus, only just completed by Chamberlain. He instructed Abbot to breathe deeply through the mouthpiece. The valves worked perfectly, and Abbot soon fell unconscious. Morton turned with a flourish and said, "Dr. Warren, *your* patient is ready."[24]

Warren worked quickly, cutting through the skin and then loosening and removing the tumor. Abbot never moved. Warren's assistant stitched the wound closed and bandaged it. Abbot slowly came to. Warren asked him if he had felt any pain. No, Abbot said, just a brief sensation of scraping on his neck, then nothing but dreams.

Warren looked up at the silent audience, tears in his eyes. "Gentlemen," he said, "this is no humbug." Bigelow added his observations, concluding, "Our craft has, once for all, been robbed of its terrors."[25]

The Second Trial

The attorney, Eddy, thought, however, that it might take a more serious operation than the removal of a surface tumor to secure a patent. Morton applied to Massachusetts General Hospital to use his mixture during an amputation, but the doctors there had had enough of Morton's secrecy regarding the nature of his anesthetic.

The surgery was scheduled for November 7. The patient, a young girl named Alice Mohan, was to have a leg amputated. She was prepared and wheeled into the operating room. As before, the rows of seats were full. Also, as before, the time for the operation came and passed with nothing happening.

In another part of the hospital, Bigelow had brought Morton a message from Warren and Dr. George

Hayward, who was now the hospital's chief of surgery. There would be no operation, Bigelow said, until Morton revealed the ingredients of his preparation.

Morton needed the operation to be performed, and he also needed the prestige that would come with the backing of Massachusetts General. He was convinced that he could still profit from the patent and from the fame he would be accorded. He therefore asked Bigelow to lead him to where Warren and Hayward waited and told them that his secret consisted of little more than sulfuric ether.

Warren and Hayward now agreed to perform the surgery, which itself went perfectly. Indeed, when Alice Mohan awoke, Warren kindly asked her if she had been asleep and if she was ready for the surgery. When she said that she was, Warren showed her amputated leg to her and said dramatically, "It is all done."[26]

The Patent Proves Worthless

Five days later, the patent was granted. For Morton, however, it turned out to be worthless. Once the news spread that the mysterious substance was only ether, doctors and dentists everywhere began using it. Morton took out a newspaper advertisement in which he threatened to sue those copying his technique, but in vain.

Not even Morton's name would be used for his discovery. When a group that included Gould, Bigelow, renowned geologist Louis Agassiz, and Dr. Oliver Wendell Holmes met with Morton on November 20 to come up with a name, Morton favored Letheon, for the Greek word for forgetfulness. But Holmes had another idea. He wrote to Morton the next day suggesting that, from the Greek words for "without feeling," "the state . . . should be called 'Anaesthesia' . . . the adjective will be 'Anaesthetic' . . . terms which will be repeated by the tongue of every civilized race of mankind."[27]

Bitter Ends

Shortly after the first demonstration of ether by William Morton in 1846, anesthesia was being hailed throughout the world as one of the greatest discoveries in history. There was considerable controversy, however, about who would get credit for the discovery, which was claimed by Morton, Horace Wells, and Charles Jackson. The battle lasted for decades and would eventually ruin the lives of all three men.

Wells failed to make much headway in the United States as the true discoverer of anesthesia. He abandoned dentistry for a time, then returned to it in New York City in 1848. By that time, however, he had become addicted to chloroform. One night, in a frenzy, he threw acid in the faces of two young women. He was arrested and jailed. Sometime late on the night of January 22, after writing a farewell note to his wife, he inhaled some smuggled chloroform and, before becoming unconscious, slashed an artery in his leg and bled to death.

Morton continued to fight for recognition. Many times he almost was granted credit for the discovery and a large cash prize by the U.S. Congress, only to be foiled by Jackson. His dentistry practice failed and so did his health. In the summer of 1868, enraged by an *Atlantic Monthly* article that gave credit to Jackson, Morton traveled to New York against his doctor's orders. He suffered a stroke, collapsed on a street corner, and died at the age of forty-eight.

Five years later, Jackson, still seeking recognition as the primary discoverer, happened to visit Morton's grave. The monument hailed Morton as the discoverer of anesthesia. Jackson fell to the ground in some sort of a fit. When he recovered, his mind was impaired. He was placed in a mental institution, never again able to communicate with family and friends. He died there in 1880.

Indeed, the news about ether anesthesia soon swept around the world and was on the lips, if not of everyone, at least of those in the medical community. Soon after it made such a powerful debut on the global stage, however, ether had a rival for the spotlight—chloroform. Together, they would at last provide the foundations for the conquest of pain.

CHAPTER 4

Chloroform and the Spread of Anesthesia

The slowness with which medicine discovered anesthesia was rivaled only by the speed with which the knowledge of this new technology spread throughout the world. Scientists soon began looking for newer, more powerful and yet safer substances, and it was not long before ether had a competitor in chloroform. The two would battle for supremacy throughout the rest of the 1800s.

Chloroform, whose chemical name is tri-chloromethane, was discovered separately and almost simultaneously by American Samuel Guthrie, German Justus von Liebig, and Frenchman Eugène Soubeiran. French chemist Jean-Baptiste-André Dumas named the chemical and described its makeup in 1834. Chloroform's ability to dull pain was well known, and Guthrie used it to relieve pain while setting broken bones. As with ether and nitrous oxide, however, no one had thought of using it to produce complete unconsciousness in surgical patients.

The man who would achieve the breakthrough was Dr. James Young Simpson. The seventh son of a baker in the Scottish town of Bathgate, Simpson early on seemed destined for greatness: He was a university student at age fourteen, a physician by twenty-one, and in January 1847, at age thirty-six, he was appointed a surgeon to Great Britain's Queen Victoria.

Simpson was one of the few doctors specializing in obstetrics at a time when the vast majority of babies were still delivered by midwives. He was disturbed by the intense pain women experienced in labor, particularly during long and difficult births.

As Simpson pondered the problem in December 1846, news of the first surgeries under ether reached Great Britain and came to the attention of Dr. Robert Liston, one of the most famous surgeons in London. Although skeptical, Liston took only two more days after reading the accounts of the American operations before making his own inhaler and undertaking a leg amputation.

When Liston's patient regained consciousness, having felt no pain, and saw his amputated leg, he fell back sobbing with relief. Liston looked at those who had gathered to watch the demonstration and said, "This Yankee dodge [trick], gentlemen, beats mesmerism hollow!"[28]

Praise from London

Less than three months after the first demonstration of anesthesia, the discovery was being praised throughout the world. This passage from the People's London Journal *of January 9, 1847, is found in* Triumph over Pain *by René Fülöp-Miller.*

Hail, happy hour that brings the glad tidings of another glorious victory. Oh, what a delight for every feeling heart to find the new year ushered in with the announcement of this noble discovery of the power to still the sense of pain. . . . It is a victory not for to-day, nor for our own time, but for another age, and all time; not for one nation, but for all nations, from generation to generation, as long as the world shall last.

The Lancet, *Britain's primary medical journal, was not quite as flowery, but equally enthusiastic:*

The discovery of Dr. Morton—more striking to the general than to the scientific mind—will undoubtedly be placed high among the blessings of human knowledge and discovery. . . . Dr. Morton deserves, if his discovery stands the test of time, the gratitude and reward of every civilized people and government upon the face of the earth.

Problems with Ether

At first, Simpson thought ether might be the answer to relieving the pain of childbirth. He experimented during the summer of 1847 but found it unsuitable. In addition to being highly flammable, its strong, pungent odor was a major problem for many pregnant women, whose condition made them highly susceptible to nausea, always dangerous during surgery because of the possibility of choking.

Simpson and his two assistants at the Edinburgh Infirmary set out to find a substitute for ether. Each evening they would gather in Simpson's home, inhaling various substances and noting the result. So reckless were their experiments that a neighbor, a Professor Miller, got into the habit of calling on Simpson before breakfast each morning to see if the trio was still alive.

On at least one occasion, it was a close call. A chemist friend of Simpson's, Lyon Playfair, suggested that he try ethyl bromide. Simpson said he would do so that very night. Playfair, though, convinced him to wait at least one more day to allow Playfair to experiment on two rabbits. When Simpson called the next day, he found the rabbits, in Playfair's words, "perfectly dead."[29]

Around the first of November, chemist David Waldie suggested Simpson try chloroform, which was being used to treat respiratory diseases and which had been shown to produce an intoxicating effect similar to that of ether. The experiment took place after supper on November 3 with Simpson, his assistants, his wife, a niece, and a family friend inhaling chloroform fumes from glass containers.

The niece was the first to feel the effects, exclaiming, "I'm an angel, oh, I'm an angel,"[30] before she fell into a deep sleep. Others in the party began laughing uncontrollably. Simpson stood on his head in the middle of the room, then crashed to the floor unconscious. When he awoke he found himself on the floor with

Thoughts on Awakening

A neighbor of James Young Simpson, one Professor Miller, fell into the habit of dropping by Simpson's home each morning to see if Simpson or his assistants were still alive after experimenting with different possible anesthetics. In November 1847, after Simpson's initial trial of chloroform, Miller had this to report, as quoted in Triumph over Pain: The Story of Anesthesia *by Robert H. Curtis.*

On awakening, Dr. Simpson's first perception was mental. "This is far stronger and better than ether," he said to himself. His second was to note that he was prostrate on the floor, and that among the friends about him there was both confusion and alarm. Hearing a noise he turned round and saw Dr. Duncan beneath a chair—his jaw dropped, his eyes staring, his head bent half under him; quite unconscious, and snoring in a most determined manner. More noise still and much motion. And then his eyes overtook Dr. Keith's feet and legs making valorous attempts to overturn the supper table or more probably to annihilate everything that was on it. [Once recovered] each expressed himself delighted with this new agent, and its inhalation was repeated many times that night.

Professor Miller finds his neighbor James Young Simpson unconscious after one of Simpson's experiments with various inhalants.

some of his companions. Others were slumped in their chairs. Some were regaining their senses; others were still snoring soundly.

The First Delivery

Less than a week later Simpson performed the first delivery using chloroform. Three hours after the patient's labor began, she was put under anesthesia. The baby was born healthy twenty-five minutes later and was taken to an adjoining room. Simpson reported that when the patient awoke, she turned round and observed to me that she had enjoyed a very comfortable sleep, and would now be more able for the work before her. In a little while she remarked that she was afraid her sleep had stopped her pains. Shortly afterward her infant was brought in by the nurse . . . and it was a matter of no small difficulty to convince the astonished mother that the labour was entirely over, and that the child presented to her was really her own living baby.[31]

Rendering a patient completely unconscious during childbirth would not be the norm, however. Such a procedure would be used in those rare cases when the labor was extremely difficult for some reason and when the mother had already borne several children, thus enlarging the birth canal and reducing the necessity for the mother to participate actively by pushing. Most of the time, chloroform was administered intermittently during labor to dull the pain of contractions but allow the mother to remain awake.

In 1847 Simpson became the first physician to use chloroform as an anesthetic during childbirth.

The Clergy Object

Simpson's use of chloroform in childbirth aroused furious opposition, not from the medical profession but from the clergy. He was denounced from pulpits throughout Britain as having gone against the will of God, who had punished Eve and all her female descendants for having tempted Adam with the forbidden fruit in the Garden of Eden.

It was written, they thundered, in Genesis 3:16, "In sorrow shalt thou bring forth children."

Simpson chose to meet scripture with scripture, citing Genesis 2:21, in which God "caused a deep sleep to fall on Adam" and then removed one of his ribs from which to make Eve. Furthermore, he said, the Hebrew word for sorrow was used later in Genesis to describe Adam's punishment for eating the fruit and could be translated as "toil" or "labor," but not "physical pain."

The clergymen were finally silenced six years later, not by Simpson's theological arguments but by the example of Queen Victoria, whose delivery of her seventh child, Prince Leopold, was aided by chloroform. Women throughout Britain, if they had hesitated before, were now quick to follow their sovereign's lead. Chloroform *à la reine*, "in the manner of the queen," became all the rage. And, since Victoria, as queen, was also head of the Church of England, the clergy had little choice but to hold their tongues no matter what they might have thought privately.

The Word Spreads

The discoveries of ether and chloroform as surgical anesthetics made one of medicine's most sought-after dreams a reality. So exciting was the news that physicians lost no time in spreading it throughout the world. Liston, after his successful amputation in London, quickly wrote to colleagues throughout Britain, "Hurrah! Rejoice! An American dentist has used the inhalation of ether to destroy sensation in his operations. In six months no operation will be performed without this previous preparation."[32] Although it would take longer than Liston predicted, it nevertheless was soon thereafter that patients far removed in both distance and culture from Boston, London, or Edinburgh were taking advantage of discoveries made in those cities.

In fact, Liston's demonstration, although it made the greatest impression in Great Britain, was not the first

The Royal Blessing

There was considerable objection to the use of chloroform during childbirth from those who believed that God had decreed women to suffer pain during the process. Such objection was effectively squelched in 1853, when Queen Victoria of Great Britain was given chloroform during the birth of her seventh child.

Given this royal blessing, chloroform quickly went from being a center of controversy to a center of fashion. Every woman wanted what the queen had been given, and it was a brave clergyman, indeed, who spoke out in opposition.

One patient of John Snow, the doctor who had administered anesthesia to the queen, wanted to know word for word what Her Majesty had said. Snow, as quoted in *The History of Surgical Anesthesia* by Thomas E. Keys, replied diplomatically, "Her Majesty asked no questions until she had breathed very much longer than you have; and if you will only go on in loyal imitation, I will tell you everything." When the woman awoke, however, Snow had already left.

After Queen Victoria used chloroform during the birth of her seventh child, pregnant women across Britain began to request the anesthetic.

to be performed there, even though it took place only five days after the news arrived. Dr. William Fraser, surgeon on the ship that had brought the first accounts of Morton's work to England, had heard the news firsthand in Boston. When the ship docked at Liverpool, Fraser went immediately to his hometown of Dumfries in Scotland. There, on December 19, one day before Liston's demonstration in London, he used ether during an operation. The almost simultaneous use of ether in England and Scotland, writes a modern historian, "indicates the gallop at which etherisation entered Great Britain."[33]

Convincing the French

The gallop slowed somewhat in France, although the news of anesthesia's discovery arrived at about the same time as in Britain. In November, Morton sent one of his inhalers to a Boston friend, Willis Fisher, who was living in Paris. Fisher first tried ether on himself, then convinced two surgeons at the Hôpital St. Louis to try it on their patients.

The operations were successful, but France's two leading surgeons, Philbert Roux and Alfred Velpeau, held back, not trusting this newfangled technique from the New World. It had been Velpeau, just a few years earlier, who had declared that pain-free surgery was something doctors dared not even hope for.

Fisher was persistent. He hounded Roux and Velpeau, bearing tales of successful anesthesia and urging them to at least give the new technique a chance. Finally, they relented, and the operation —a month after the first demonstration in France— was equally successful.

Robert Liston discovered that ether serves as an effective anesthesia for major surgeries after conducting an amputation using the concoction in 1846.

The two formerly reluctant surgeons quickly became ardent enthusiasts. Roux called anesthesia "a glorious victory for mankind," and Velpeau said, "Even the most incredulous must bow before the power of facts."[34]

Germany, too, had its skeptics. One surgeon, an avowed atheist, declared he would rather resort to prayer to relieve pain instead of anesthesia. But after Dr. J.F. Heyfelder performed a painless surgery on January 24, German doctors quickly agreed with Dr. Johann Dieffenbach, who wrote:

> Pain . . . has had to retreat before the power of man's mind, before the advance of ether vapor. This discovery has gone far to rob death of its terrors, for we dread the pain of death more than we dread death itself. Does not our imagination lead us to fear the agony of a major surgical operation more than we fear death, so that we would do our utmost to avoid it? Now we can avoid this agony, to our wonder and admiration.[35]

The Death Rate Increases

As helpful as it was in alleviating pain, anesthesia did not increase the success rate of surgery. In fact, the number of deaths after surgery increased in the twenty years after anesthesia's discovery. This was because, with their patients unconscious, doctors were able to perform longer, more complex, and more invasive procedures than before. These operations carried with them greatly increased risks of infection. It was only after the introduction of antiseptic techniques by Dr. Joseph Lister in 1867 that the mortality rate fell.

The rising death rate from surgery, however, did little to stop the use of anesthesia from spreading worldwide. Later, in 1847, both Nikolai Pirogoff in Russia and a Dr. Schuh in Austria pioneered its use in their countries. From Europe, it spread east and south. By the end of the year, anesthesia had been used in South Africa, Australia, and Japan. Both ether and chloroform were relatively easy to manufacture, and before long

A patient inhales chloroform as an apparatus emits an antiseptic spray. In 1867 Joseph Lister introduced antiseptic substances and surgical techniques to the operating room.

missionaries were even taking supplies of anesthetics deep into jungles and high into remote mountain ranges and performing operations on the people they ministered to there.

These trailblazers in anesthesia chose between ether and chloroform largely based on their country of origin. Chloroform had been first used in Scotland and remained the anesthesia of choice there and throughout most of mainland Europe. Ether had gotten off to a head start in England because of Liston's demonstration and was the favorite of physicians there. And, with the rapid expansion of the British Empire during the second half of the 1800s, ether also was the choice of surgeons in such British dominions as South Africa, Australia, and New Zealand.

Jealousy in the United States

Strangely, acceptance of the new technique was slower to catch on in the country of its birth, the United

States, than across the ocean. One reason was that the discovery had been made and demonstrated in Boston.

Ever since Colonial times, Boston had been regarded —by Bostonians most of all—as the center of learning and culture in the United States. Doctors elsewhere thus tended to be jealous of and resist most Bostonian innovations. Consequently, pronouncements such as one by Dr. John Warren praising Massachusetts General Hospital as the spot where "here was first demonstrated one of the most glorious truths of science"[36] were bound to draw negative reactions elsewhere.

In Philadelphia, for instance, the *Medical Examiner* called the news of anesthesia a "swindle" and "quackery" and added, "We should not consider it entitled to the least notice, but we perceive, by the Boston *Medical and Surgical Journal*, that prominent members

An illustration depicts the use of chloroform during an operation in Afghanistan in 1885. News of the effectiveness of anesthesia spread rapidly throughout the world.

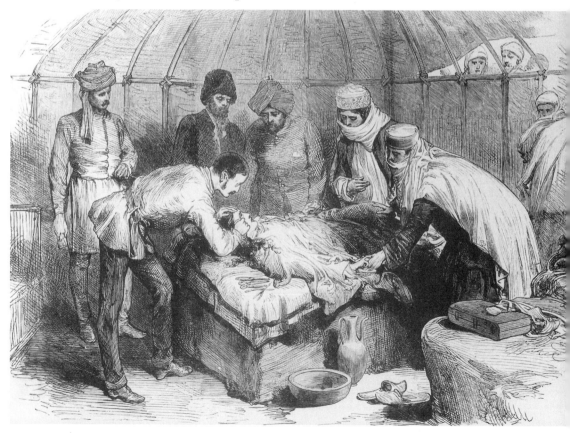

of the profession in that city have been caught in its meshes."[37]

The Great Question

Newspapers in New York City and New Orleans were equally hostile. Consequently, many doctors—and their patients—hesitated to use anesthesia. At the first annual meeting in Philadelphia of the American Medical Association, the Committee on Surgery reported:

> The great question, which still divides medical opinion, is: Can the annulling of pain by anesthetic agents be produced without risk to life, or is the hazard so inconsiderable as to justify their employment in all cases where it is desirable to prevent the pain of surgical operations?[38]

The report went on to say that many surgeons "would restrict the use of these agents [anesthetics] to severe operations . . . while a small proportion of the profession still object altogether to anaesthetics as dangerous and hurtful."[39]

Although a prominent Philadelphia hospital boasted late in 1847 of never having allowed an operation under anesthesia, the prospect of painless surgery was one that doctors and patients could not long resist. By 1850 the use of anesthesia was commonplace in virtually every hospital in the United States. Expressions of gratitude and thanksgiving came from everywhere—doctors, universities, kings, and presidents—but perhaps none was as eloquent as the action of a mother in Scotland, who was so thankful for the use of chloroform during a delivery that she named her baby girl Anesthesia.

CHAPTER 5

New Drugs, Deliveries, and Deliverers

The discovery of anesthesia and its rapid acceptance opened the gates for a flood of subsequent improvements. Now that science finally realized that surgical anesthesia was possible, research leaped forward. The decades following the initial discovery saw a steady march of progress—newer and safer drugs, more sophisticated methods of administering them, and the growth of an entire medical specialty.

Doctors quickly realized that their methods of administering anesthetics were too crude to allow for precise dosing of the anesthetic. Sometimes delivery consisted only of holding a handkerchief over the patient's mouth and nose. Another popular method was to cover the patient's face with a wire mask covered with gauze and then drip anesthetic onto the gauze, but this, too, was imprecise. The result could be a lethal overdose. The first deaths from overdoses of ether were reported in March 1847, and the first death from chloroform occurred only two months after its first use. Clearly, some device was needed to regulate the dose of anesthetic administered.

The pioneer in the area of anesthetic delivery apparatuses was John Snow, an English physician who eventually devoted his entire medical career to anesthesia.

In 1847 he invented an ether inhaler that ensured an exact, steady, and predictable mixture of ether vapor and air. Snow later showed the importance of maintaining ether at a constant temperature to control the amount of vapor given off and modified his inhaler accordingly. He also worked with chloroform—determining that a ratio of four parts chloroform to ninety-six parts air provided optimum safety—and devised an inhaler that produced such a mixture.

Anesthesia Machines

The major advance in inhalation came toward the end of the 1800s with the development of anesthetic machines that delivered gases from pressurized canisters through a series of valves. Best known was the

Nineteenth-century anesthesia delivery devices were crude and imprecise. With this gauze-covered mask, for example, patients breathed anesthesia dripped onto the gauze.

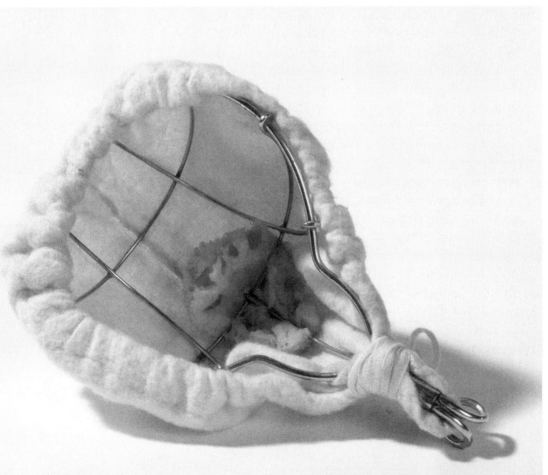

machine developed by British physician Henry Boyle, who, in 1917, devised reducing valves to convert the high pressure of gases inside canisters to a steady flow through a breathing apparatus. This type of device, with constant modifications, would remain the basic method of delivering inhalation anesthesia into the twenty-first century.

The breathing mask, however, still did not deliver the anesthetic mixture as precisely as desired, mainly because making the mask airtight was difficult. The answer was a technique called endotracheal anesthesia, in which the gas is delivered through a tube inserted in the patient's throat directly into the lungs. In addition to the precision of flow, it has the advantage of using less anesthetic since the gas reaches the lungs more quickly and is therefore more quickly absorbed into the bloodstream. It also prevents the mouth and throat from being irritated by the anesthetic.

Endotracheal anesthesia also allows the use of a breathing machine, or ventilator, to supply oxygen to the patient during surgery. Only with such an aid to respiration is chest surgery possible since opening the chest cavity would normally cause the lungs to collapse because of a difference in pressure.

Early Intubation

Although the application of anesthesia through endotracheal intubation did not take place until 1852, the technique of using a tube to maintain artificial respiration had been known for centuries. The Belgian physician Vesalius included in his anatomy book Fabrica *in 1543 a description of a tracheotomy performed on a dog. This excerpt is found in* The History of Surgical Anesthesia *by Thomas E. Keys.*

But that life may in a manner of speaking be restored to the animal, an opening must be attempted in the trunk of the trachea, into which a tube of reed or cane should be put; you will then blow into this, so that the lung may rise again and the animal take in air. Indeed, with a slight breath in the case of this living animal the lung will swell to the full extent of the thoracic cavity, and the heart become strong and exhibit a wondrous variety of motions. So, with the lung inflated once and a second time, you examine the motion of the heart by sight and touch as much as you wish.

New Drugs

Just as the delivery devices underwent rapid evolution, so too did the anesthetic drugs themselves. Chloroform developed wide popularity after its first use by Simpson, but it lost its appeal when it was discovered that it could cause the heart to stop in some cases and in others could remain in the liver at harmful levels. There were also problems with ether, which kept patients unconscious longer than doctors liked, and with nitrous oxide, which took too long to work. Ethyl chloride was developed as an anesthetic in the 1890s, and trichloroethylene was created in 1911. Related to chloroform, both were first thought to be safe but later displayed similar toxicity.

Other substances were developed with various results and various drawbacks. One of the most successful was cyclopropane, first developed in 1929 and in general use by 1935. It works very quickly and its chemical makeup is such that it does not irritate the linings of the lungs or throat. The complexity of the manufacturing process, however, makes cyclopropane expensive, and its speed of operation increases the risk of overdosage.

Two of the more recent popular drugs have been halothane, first used in 1956, and isoflurane, developed in 1965. Both work rapidly and have limited side effects, but both also tend to reduce blood pressure and suppress breathing. Despite these drawbacks, halothane and isoflurane still are widely used inhalation agents, although close monitoring of patients is essential.

The Hypodermic Syringe

Doctors knew that inhalation agents took effect after reaching the bloodstream by way of the lungs. Why not, they reasoned, inject the drugs directly? This method was made possible by the nearly simultaneous invention in 1853 of the syringe by Charles Pravaz in France and the hollow needle by Alexander Wood in Scotland. Together, they formed the hypodermic syringe.

At first, doctors tried the new method—intravenous anesthesia—using the old standbys, ether and chloroform, but for some reason these anesthetics were not as effective as they were when inhaled. It was not until 1903 that a new family of drugs appeared when

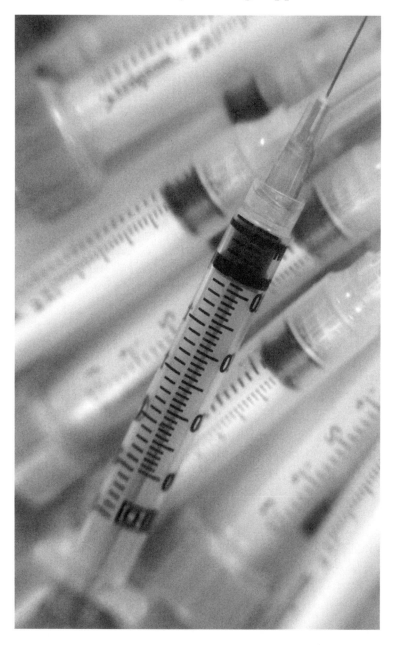

The invention of the hypodermic syringe in 1853 made it possible to inject anesthetic drugs directly into the bloodstream.

German chemists Emil Fischer and Joseph von Mering developed the first barbiturates. They were experimenting on animals with various derivatives of barbituric acid when they accidentally discovered that one, diethylbarbituric acid, caused unconsciousness. The early barbiturates, such as Veronal, Luminal, and Nembutal, were too slow to be used for general anesthesia and were employed mainly to relax patients before inhalants were applied.

Later, however, new barbiturates—Evipal and Thiopentone—came on the scene. They worked very quickly. Patients given Thiopentone often were unconscious before they could count to ten. Side effects seemed to be very minimal, but research later showed that barbiturates could adversely affect both heart rate and circulation. Their other disadvantage was that, unlike the newer inhalation agents, they took longer to work their way out of the body.

Not all intravenous anesthetics are barbiturates. The benzodiazepine class of drugs came into use in 1961 as a relaxant prior to administration of other agents. Etomidate appeared in 1971 and propofol in 1977. So effective was propofol that in the 1980s it was frequently the only anesthetic used for major surgeries, though it is now used mainly as a first step in the anesthesia process.

Local Anesthesia

More or less at the same time that researchers were working to develop general anesthetics—that is, agents that produced narcosis, or complete unconsciousness, others were looking for ways to anesthetize only the area of the body to be operated on. Such a "local" anesthetic, doctors reasoned, would reduce the risk of fatalities, reduce adverse side effects and provide anesthesia in cases—such as eye surgery—in which it was beneficial to have the patient conscious.

The substance researchers focused on was cocaine. In 1860 chemist Albert Niemann had succeeded in iso-

A New Anesthetic Blooms

The history of science is full of accounts of how important discoveries were made by accident. One such fortunate happenstance led to the identification of the anesthetic ethylene.

In the early 1920s a gardener in Chicago, Illinois, noticed that many of the carnations he was growing in a greenhouse had withered and died. He also noticed a peculiar smell and found a leaky natural gas pipe in the lighting system.

He held a healthy carnation next to the leak and the blossom closed as if going to sleep. When he took the flower out into fresh air, it opened. When he held another flower next to the leak for an extended period of time, it died.

Two botanists at the University of Chicago heard about the mysterious action of the gas and started experimenting with natural gas on various plants. These experiments, in turn, led zoologists Arno Luckhardt and J.B. Carter to begin similar work with animals. In 1923 they were able to isolate ethylene, and it went into use the same year. Less flammable and pungent than ether, ethylene continued in general use into the 1970s.

lating cocaine from the leaves of the coca plant native to South America. He noted during his experiments that cocaine, when taken orally, numbed the tongue, but it would be more than twenty years before its potential as an anesthetic would be realized.

In 1884 Bohemian-born Carl Koller, while studying in Austria to be an eye doctor, sought to find a method other than general anesthesia, using ether or chloroform, for use in eye surgery. He knew that cocaine produced numbness on the tongue and experimented by placing drops of a cocaine solution in the eye of a frog, leaving it insensitive to the touch.

Cocaine's ability to penetrate the membranes covering the eye and the insides of the nose, mouth, and throat made it ideal for surgery in these areas. The technique is called topical anesthesia because the anesthetic is administered directly on the surface to be operated on.

Doctors knew cocaine could be effective in ways other than as a topical anesthetic, and they reasoned that, as with barbiturates, the hypodermic syringe might be the answer. Soon after Koller's discovery,

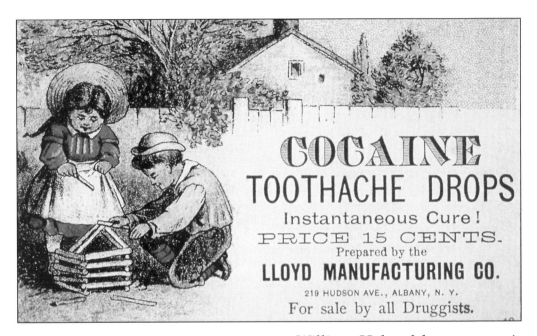

An advertisement for cocaine toothache drops illustrates the widespread use of cocaine as a topical anesthetic beginning in the late nineteenth century.

American surgeon William Halsted began experimenting with cocaine injections. His first major discovery was that injecting cocaine into the main trunk of a nerve deadened all the nerves leading from it. In this way, a single injection could anesthetize an area such as a leg or the jaw. This method became known as regional or conduction anesthesia.

Corning's Experiment

The discovery that a major nerve and all those branching from it could be deadened soon led to experiments aimed at relieving chronic pain caused by diseased nerves. An American researcher, James Leonard Corning, experimented on a dog by injecting cocaine into an area just outside the dura, the fluid-filled covering of the spinal cord. Although the drug only was injected near the spinal cord, the dog soon lost all feeling in its hind legs.

Corning's technique became known as epidural, meaning "outside the dura," anesthesia. In the decades that followed, doctors came to deliver a variety of anesthetics in this way. The technique was especially useful in childbirth since it avoided the dangers and side effects of general anesthesia and enabled the mother to stay awake in order to witness the birth.

The epidural technique was taken to the next level after a German doctor, Heinrich Quincke, showed that the dura could be punctured without damage to the spinal cord. His countryman August Bier took the next step, injecting cocaine into the sac of fluid surrounding the spinal cord. The technique, known as spinal anesthesia as opposed to epidural, requires far less anesthetic and is longer lasting.

Infiltration Anesthesia

At about the same time as epidural and spinal anesthesia were developed, another technique—infiltration anesthesia—was introduced. Large amounts of cocaine had produced fatal reactions in some patients, and many doctors were fearful of spinal anesthesia, particularly for minor surgery. German surgeon Carl

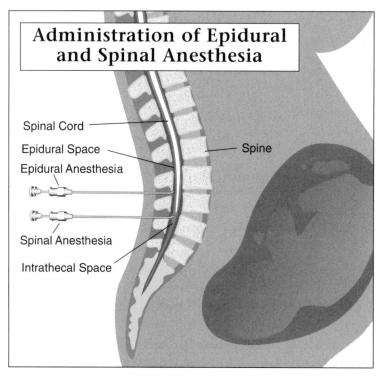

Administration of Epidural and Spinal Anesthesia

Spinal Cord

Epidural Space

Epidural Anesthesia

Spine

Spinal Anesthesia

Intrathecal Space

Schleich discovered the method of making multiple injections of diluted cocaine around the area to be operated on. Infiltration anesthesia became highly popular because it avoided some of the side effects of spinal or epidural anesthesia, such as headaches and nausea.

Cocaine, however, proved to be a dangerous drug. Not only did it cause some fatalities due to cardiac arrest and have unpleasant side effects ranging from nausea to irritation of membranes, but it also proved to be highly addictive. It was still common around 1900 for researchers to experiment on themselves. Several, including Halsted, became cocaine addicts from injecting themselves, and some patients who received repeated large doses found themselves similarly addicted.

In response to this problem, chemists sought to manufacture a synthetic form of cocaine that would have the same anesthetic effect but with less danger. The first to appear was procaine, developed in 1905 by German chemist Alfred Einhorn. Although the effects of procaine were shorter-lived than those of cocaine, it was discovered that adding a substance called epinephrine prolonged anesthesia by constricting blood vessels and thus slowing the absorption of procaine into the body. Procaine, which went under the trade name Novocain, would remain the most popular local anesthetic until the development of its cousin, lidocaine, in the 1950s.

Curare

Cocaine was not the only dangerous drug coming out of South America to find a home in modern anesthesia. Another such substance, curare, although not itself technically an anesthetic, greatly aided surgeons by reducing the amount of other drugs required. Curare is a muscle relaxant, and for centuries native hunters had coated spears and arrowheads with this substance in order to kill their quarry by causing the muscles used for breathing to stop working. Research showed, however, that carefully controlled amounts of curare could

Curare Is First Described

The first description of the poison curare, much later to become a valuable anesthetic used to relax muscles during surgery, was made in 1751 by Charles-Marie de La Condamine. La Condamine headed an expedition to South America organized by the French Academy of Sciences. Although primarily a mathematician, La Condamine was a keen observer. His description of curare is found in Arrows of Mercy *by Philip Smith.*

The *Yamesos* [a tribe in the Amazon River basin] propel by the breath small arrows of wood to a distance of thirty or forty paces, and rarely miss their target. . . . They cover the points of these little arrows, as well as those used with the bow, with a poison so active that, when it is fresh, it will kill in less than a minute any animal whose blood it has entered. Although we had our fowling pieces [firearms used to hunt birds], we hardly ate anything killed in any other way than by these darts. . . . There is no danger from this; the poison only kills if it enters the blood; but it is no less mortal to man than to animals.

be safe and very helpful during certain surgeries in humans.

Even with anesthesia, abdominal surgery had always been difficult because large quantities of inhalant anesthetics were needed to relax the strong muscles in that area. In 1942 Canadian surgeons Harold Griffin and Enid Johnson performed the first operation using a combination of curare and cyclopropane. Far less cyclopropane was needed than otherwise would have been the case.

The successful use of curare demonstrates how the various components of anesthesia are interdependent. Curare makes certain surgeries more practical. In turn, surgery using curare is possible only because endotracheal anesthesia and the ventilator allow doctors to keep the patient breathing if the chest muscles are too relaxed for breathing to occur naturally.

Balanced Anesthesia

The combination of curare with another anesthetic also demonstrates the principle of "balanced anesthesia." Despite decades of research, medical science has yet to find the perfect anesthetic. Every drug—whether inhaled, taken orally, applied topically, or administered intravenously—has drawbacks. Some are not powerful enough for certain surgeries. Others are too powerful and are thus dangerous except in combination with others, which allow smaller quantities to be used. Some drugs work better at the start of the anesthesia process but not for the entire procedure. Others are excellent at maintaining unconsciousness or insensitivity but are less effective at the beginning. Virtually all have at least one unpleasant side effect. Medicine's answer has been balanced anesthesia—using anesthetics in combination with one another or with other substances and in proper sequences to provide both the desired level of anesthesia with the maximum of safety.

The concept of balanced anesthesia dates from the 1860s, when a committee of physicians in England suggested that surgeons use chloroform to render patients unconscious, then switch to ether to maintain unconsciousness. About the same time, a concoction of alcohol, chloroform, and ether in a 1:2:3 ratio—the ACE mixture—became popular and remained so for most of the century.

Anesthesia Levels

In 1911 Ohio doctor George Washington Crile developed a method of administering both a general and a local anesthetic during the same operation. However, the modern concept of balanced anesthesia was developed in 1926 by John S. Lundy at the Mayo Clinic in Minnesota. Lundy taught that each stage of an operation requires a different level of anesthesia depending on the desired outcome.

For example, a patient might be given a drug orally or intravenously to reduce anxiety, followed by intravenous anesthetic to bring about initial unconsciousness and muscle relaxation. Once "asleep," the patient might be intubated for endotracheal anesthesia, something difficult if not impossible on a fully conscious patient.

A combination of inhalant agents—perhaps nitrous oxide, oxygen, and isoflurane—would maintain unconsciousness. At the end of the surgery, drugs might be given to reverse the muscle relaxant, allowing the patient to breathe normally. Depending on the surgery, yet another drug might be used to limit postoperative pain.

In 1950 the different aspects of anesthesia were first divided into formal classifications—relaxation; analgesia, or pain relief; and narcosis, or unconsciousness. Two additional classifications were added later—amnesia, in which a patient might experience pain at the time of surgery but have no memory of it later; and attenuation, or suppression of natural reflexes.

The increasing complexity of both anesthetics and ways to administer them quickly brought an end to the time when surgeons could do the job themselves or leave it to a minimally trained assistant. Anesthesia at this point gave rise to an entire medical specialty— anesthesiology.

Dr. John Snow

The man who truly could be called the first anesthesiologist, long before the term was coined in 1902 by American surgeon M.J. Seifert, was Dr. John Snow. Snow's skill in administering ether brought him to the attention of the great Robert Liston, and from then on, writes one biographer, "the ether practice in London came exclusively to Dr. Snow."[40] Not only did he develop better inhalers, but he also wrote the first definitive book on anesthesia in 1858.

Snow also established some of the practices that led to anesthesiology as a distinct specialty. He emphasized close monitoring of patients' breathing and pulse. He also maintained meticulous records of operations, although this practice was not generally adopted until the 1890s.

For many years, the training of anesthesiologists was closely tied to that of surgeons, with all courses dealing with anesthetics and their delivery listed under departments of surgery. It was not until the 1930s that the first separate anesthesiology departments were established in medical schools. In the decades since, the body of knowledge in anesthesiology and the complexity of surgery have increased to the point where anesthesiology has been divided into subsets and even subsets of subsets. For example, cardiac anesthesiologists specialize in heart operations, and pediatric cardiac anesthesiologists deal only with anesthesia during heart surgery in children.

A Clear Distinction

Although all medical professionals who administer anesthetics are highly trained, a clear distinction exists between anesthesiologists and anesthetists. Anesthesiologists are qualified physicians who have graduated from a medical school and have undergone years

The Mystery of Anesthesia

Despite all the research, nobody has been able to explain how all general anesthetics—those that cause the unconscious state known as narcosis—actually work. Instead, the various schools of thought concerning general anesthesia are combined in the multiple agent–specific (MAS) theory. Proponents of the MAS theory reject the notion that a single mechanism is the root cause of anesthesia.

MAS proponents say that all other theories have too many exceptions and that different anesthetics operate in different ways. Their contention is backed up by research showing that encephalograms—measurements of the brain's electrical activity—show different patterns when different classes of anesthetics are applied.

Yet although scientists who subscribe to the MAS theory agree that there are different mechanisms that can bring about general anesthesia, they still cannot agree on what those mechanisms are. Joan Kendig, a professor at the Stanford University School of Medicine, is quoted by journalist Mary Brophy Marcus in her *U.S. News & World Report* article titled "How Does Anesthesia Work?" as saying, "There are as many theories about where anesthetics are acting as there are researchers in the field." The vast majority of patients, however, are happy enough to leave the theories to the scientists. It is enough for them that anesthetics work and work safely.

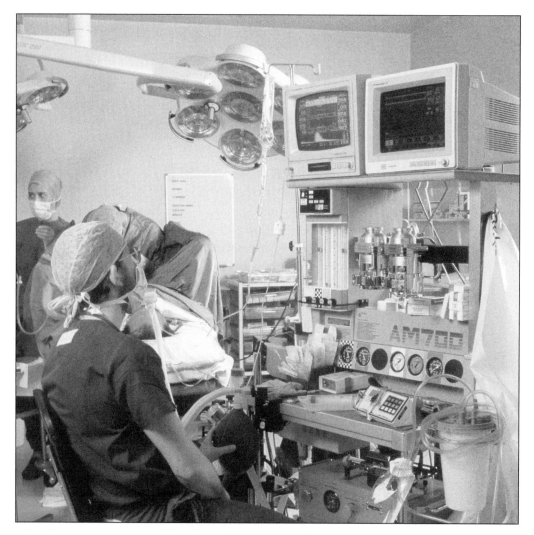

of subsequent specialized training. Anesthetists are technicians who administer anesthetics under the supervision of an anesthesiologist.

Most anesthetists are registered nurses, and they form an increasingly important part of the medical team. This nursing specialty, which formed its own society in 1931, gained wide recognition during World War II when doctors were in short supply. Today in the United States, an estimated 65 percent of all anesthesia is administered by nurse anesthetists under the supervision of anesthesiologists.

An anesthetist monitors the condition of a patient under general anesthesia. Anesthetists are registered nurses who work under the supervision of an anesthesiologist.

CHAPTER 6

Mixed Blessing

Shortly after the news of the discovery of ether reached London, the *People's Journal* trumpeted, "We have conquered pain."[41] A few months later, however, a fifteen-year-old girl named Hannah Greener died after receiving chloroform for a routine toenail operation. Doctors soon realized that the weapons with which they sought to free their patients from pain could kill the very people they sought to help.

New drugs and new techniques have improved the effectiveness of anesthesia but also have multiplied the risks. As a result, anesthesiologists have fought a constant battle to minimize those risks. "Patient safety is not a fad," says Ellison C. Pierce of Harvard Medical School. "Patient safety is an ongoing necessity. And it must be constantly sustained by research, training, and daily application in the workplace."[42]

Many of the dangers of undergoing anesthesia have nothing to do with the drugs themselves nor with the quantity in which they are given. According to the American Society of Anesthesiologists' Closed Claims Project, which has tracked malpractice damage claims since 1984, 6 percent of all reported complications involve physical damage to the airway while inserting the endotracheal tube. Such injuries tend not to be severe, only rarely resulting in a patient's death.

The area most affected by airway damage is the larynx, sometimes called the voice box, with paralysis of the vocal cords the most common injury. The other primary injury sites are the esophagus and trachea, mostly as the result of difficulty inserting an endotracheal tube. Other damage occurs to patients' noses and to the joints of the upper and lower jaw.

Dental Injuries

The Closed Claims Project does not factor dental injuries into its airway damage statistics, but such incidents are common. Intubation materials inserted through the mouth have metal parts, and there is a chance of injury to the teeth and gums if sufficient care is not taken. Such damage is more likely in children, smaller adults, and in those with bridges, retainers, or other permanent dental fixtures. Companies that manufacture intubation materials have tried to make them as compact as possible, keep metal parts to a minimum, and eliminate any rough edges, but the key to preventing such physical injury is a greater degree of caution on the part of the people who insert them.

Another type of physical damage can occur when needles puncture the dura covering the spinal cord. Direct harm to the cord itself is rare. It is much more common

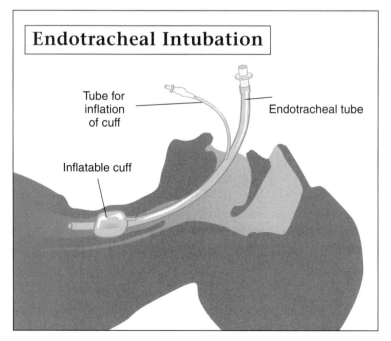

Endotracheal Intubation

Tube for inflation of cuff

Endotracheal tube

Inflatable cuff

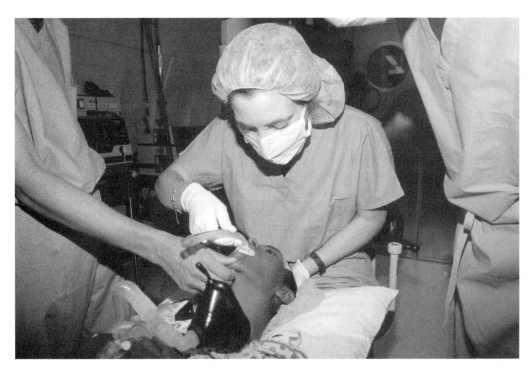

An anesthesiologist inserts a tube into the larynx of a patient to help administer general anesthesia. The larynx is the area most likely to be injured during intubation.

for spinal fluid to leak through the puncture. This results in a lowering of pressure within the spinal column, resulting in a severe headache to the patient. If the headache fails to respond to traditional pain medications, it is a sign that the puncture has not healed itself; the physician may employ a "blood patch," injecting the patient's own blood into the puncture site to create a clot.

Other injections of local anesthesia carry their own dangers. For instance, doctors giving a cocaine-derivative nerve block to the brachial plexus—the bundle of nerves serving the chest, shoulder, and arm—must be careful that the needle does not puncture the lung, which is located near the site. If this happens, a collapsed lung usually results, necessitating a chest tube to maintain air pressure.

Positioning

A more general danger for surgical patients is the risk of nerve damage if the way their bodies are positioned places pressure on certain nerves. Although positioning involves neither anesthetics nor delivery mechanisms, it falls under the anesthesiologist's responsibility. Ironically, most of the nerve damage from poor positioning happens only because anesthesia enables surgeries to last for longer periods. Exactly why nerve injury through mispositioning occurs is not known. Moreover, such injury may occur in some patients even though precautions with padding have been taken. Fortunately for the patient, such damage usually heals itself in weeks or months.

Of course, from the earliest days of anesthesia up to fairly modern times, the greatest danger was from the drugs themselves. Anesthetics are inherently harmful; many are potent poisons. The vast majority, when given in an overdose, can cause severe permanent injury or death.

Anesthetics can be harmful in several ways. The most common early problem with inhalants was that the mixture of anesthetic with air provided insufficient oxygen, which could cause death or brain damage. The situation improved when doctors were able to mix anesthetics with pure oxygen instead of room air, but ensuring adequate oxygen remains the anesthesiologist's primary task.

When Hannah Greener died in 1848, it was not directly from chloroform but rather from the nausea it produced. She, and many others subsequently, died after surgery by choking on their own vomit. Nausea immediately after surgery is one of the most common side effects of general anesthesia and is the reason surgeons usually ask their patients to fast for twelve or more hours prior to the operation.

Fibrillation

Deaths from chloroform—besides those resulting from inhaling vomit—began in the late 1840s, but no one knew what the problem was until 1911, when Alfred Goodman Levy showed that chloroform could affect the rhythm of the heart. The rapid, irregular beating of the heart, known as fibrillation, led to cardiac arrest—stopping of the heart—and death. Because of fibrillation and other dangers, use of chloroform as a general anesthetic virtually ended in the early 1900s. Newer drugs, however, have been shown to cause heart arrhythmia as well. Local anesthetics of the cocaine family, in particular, can cause heart problems in large doses. In addition, some drugs—such as adrenaline— given along with local anesthetics can cause the heart to speed up.

Medicine has developed to the point, however, where the risk of serious injury or death from anesthesia is very small—and getting smaller all the time. In the 1950s 1 out of every 3,000 to 4,000 patients undergoing surgery died from complications involving general anesthesia. Now, the death rate is estimated to be about 1 in 250,000.

Such progress has been made in patient safety not because of newer drugs and more sophisticated delivery mechanisms. Indeed, those factors have served only to make anesthesia much more complex than in the 1950s. Rather, the difference has come about by paying more attention to the human element—both in training the people who tend to patients and looking after the patients themselves.

Human Error

Overdoses of anesthetics almost always occur because of human error. In the early days, doctors had little idea of what a proper dose was and had no accurate way to regulate the dosage even if they had known. Furthermore, the administration of anesthetics was frequently left to surgeons' assistants, who had little or no training. Country doctors sometimes called on bystanders, even members of the patients' families, to apply more ether or chloroform.

Many of the risks of anesthesia can be avoided simply by the anesthesiologist talking with the patient before surgery, a practice that has become commonplace only since about 1950. Such preoperative assessments can turn up details that may determine the type and amounts of anesthetics to be used. If a patient has a history of lung disease, for example, muscle relaxants that could impair breathing might be limited. If there are heart problems, stimulants such as adrenaline might be avoided. Anesthesiologists need to learn as much as possible from the patient beforehand since there will be no chance to question an unconscious patient if a situation arises that requires administration of a drug whose use was unanticipated.

The Importance of Monitoring

Closely monitoring patients during surgery can prevent small problems from turning into disasters. As early as the 1840s John Snow wrote that the "pulse was pretty good"[43] in one of his patients. The trouble was that for much of the history of anesthesia, patients have not had people as capable as Snow looking after them. Often it was the surgeon who administered anesthesia

The Danger of Chloroform

Although chloroform had several advantages over ether as a general anesthetic, it had one very large drawback. Many more people died during surgery from chloroform than from ether, their hearts suddenly stopping.

The Glasgow Committee, formed by the British Medical Association in 1875, concluded that chloroform was much more dangerous to the heart. In 1889, however, the Hyderabad Commission conducted experiments on dogs that showed no effects on the heart until after breathing had stopped.

Other commissions reached various conclusions, and it was not until 1911 that Alfred Goodman Levy, as reported in The Evolution of Anesthesia *by M.H. Armstrong Davison,*

communicated a note to the Physiological Society describing a hitherto unrecognized form of sudden cardiac failure which occurred in cats under chloroform, and stating that he had, acting upon a suggestion made by Professor Cushny, looked for and found ventricular fibrillation in such cases. At the same time he showed that an exactly similar form of death could be reproduced by injecting small doses of adrenaline into the vein of a cat lightly anaesthetized with chloroform. These observations became the starting-point of a series of experiments elucidating the conditions under which ventricular fibrillation occurs, and showing that it happens only in light chloroform anaesthesia, never in full or deep anaesthesia.

and who then was too busy with the operation to take more than an occasional glance at the patient.

Snow encouraged doctors to employ trained assistants to monitor patients' pulse rate, respiration, and the pupils of the eye. According to Ellison C. Pierce, monitoring a century later was not much different, the only addition being a blood-pressure indicator.

The big change occurred in the 1980s, and it was spurred by a television program. On April 22, 1982, the program *20/20* broadcast a segment titled "The Deep Sleep." The program stated that six thousand patients would die that year from "a danger they never knew existed—mistakes in administering anesthesia."[44] The mistakes recounted in the program included improper use of anesthetic delivery machines, poor equipment design, and poor patient monitoring due to an insufficient number of personnel.

Improved Equipment

Anesthesiologists responded in several ways, one of which was to develop better monitoring equipment. As a result, doctors have been afforded several valuable new tools in the twenty years or so since the program aired. One of the most significant is the pulse oximeter, which accurately measures how much oxygen a patient receives. The pulse oximeter is attached to a finger or toe by means of a clip. By shining red and infrared light through the nail, the device is able—despite differences in skin tissue and pigment and no matter how much light is in the operating room—to measure, heartbeat by heartbeat, the level of oxygen in the blood.

A second major advance has been the capnometer or capnograph. Capnography, or the measurement of carbon dioxide being exhaled by the patient, had been practiced in some hospitals since the 1950s as a tool to assess lung ventilation, but techniques were crude. The newer machines draw exhaled air into a chamber where it is exposed to infrared light. The amounts of

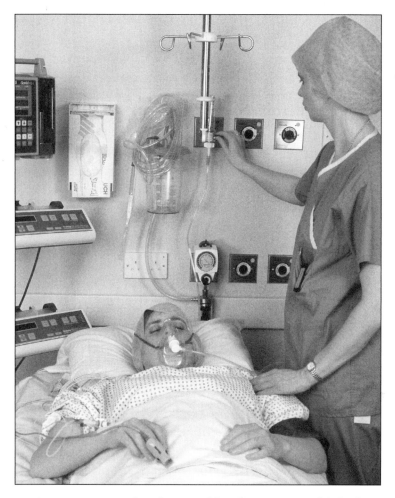

A nurse adjusts the oxygen flowmeter connected to a patient's face mask, and a pulse oximeter attached to her finger measures the oxygen level in her blood.

various gases can be detected by the rate at which they absorb the light. Even more precise capnography is possible with mass spectrometers, but these devices are expensive, making them unaffordable for all but the largest hospitals. The capnometer immediately tells the anesthesiologist whether the endotracheal tube has been inserted properly into the trachea (which leads to the lungs) instead of into the esophagus (which leads to the stomach), an easy mistake to make.

Other Advances

Several other devices have become available to monitor surgical patients under anesthesia. Automatic blood pressure machines deliver constant information. Body temperature is measured, not on the surface, but internally, from a tiny sensor located on the breathing tube. Another helpful device can measure the impulses being received by peripheral nerves, those on the outer edge of the nervous system. The anesthesiologist can thus tell the extent to which the anesthetic has taken effect and how quickly it has worn off. The latter is sometimes a good measure of whether it is safe to remove the breathing tube.

Other major improvements have been made in the machines that deliver anesthetics. Earlier machines provided ample room for error. Hoses and fittings delivering different gasses often were the same size and color. On some older machines, valves were not standardized; on one machine, the amount of anesthetic could be increased by turning a valve to the right whereas another machine required the valve to be turned to the left to accomplish the same thing.

Today's machines have fail-safe devices to prevent, as much as possible, human and mechanical error. Hoses are prominently labeled, and their fittings match only the correct canisters of gas. Alarms sound if a hose comes loose. Meters calibrating the flow of anesthetics have been made more accurate and easier to read.

Postoperative Care

Patient care after surgery has likewise improved. According to Pierce, postoperative recovery rooms were primitive in the 1950s and were not in use at all in Europe. Today, patients are monitored with many of the same machines used during surgery. Only after the major effects of the anesthesia have worn off are patients allowed to either go home or be taken to a regular hospital room.

Impressive as the technological advances in anesthesia monitoring are, they are of little value without properly trained personnel. The television program 20/20, in addition to discussing the lack of sophistication in monitoring, also pointed out that in many hospitals there were not enough people to handle the surgical caseload. For example, at one point in the program a reporter was told of cases in New York City in which two anesthesiologists covered five operating rooms at once. When asked how they did it, the person said, "Well, they run quickly and pray a lot."[45]

20/20's revelations also led to an effort by anesthesiologists to establish a comprehensive and ongoing program to study and improve patient safety. A conference in Boston in 1984 had two major outcomes, the first of which was establishing the Anesthesia Patient Safety Foundation (APSF). The APSF publishes a widely read newsletter containing timely articles on safety issues and also awards grants of more than $1.3 million for research in anesthesia safety.

Anesthesia Standards

The other major result of the Boston conference was the establishment by the American Society of Anesthesiologists (ASA) of what are considered the basic standards for patient monitoring. Although the standards

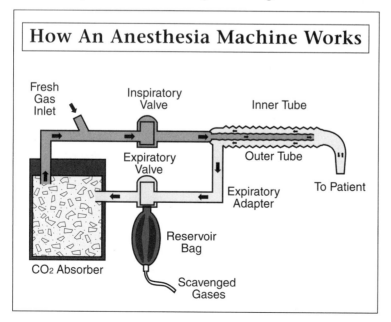

How An Anesthesia Machine Works

Fresh Gas Inlet

Inspiratory Valve

Inner Tube

Expiratory Valve

Outer Tube

Expiratory Adapter

To Patient

Reservoir Bag

CO$_2$ Absorber

Scavenged Gases

were suggestions at the time, they have been given the force of law in many states. Indeed, some states have adopted standards more stringent than the ASA standards.

Generally, such standards address three major areas: preanesthesia care, basic monitoring during surgery, and postanesthesia care. The first area calls for doctors to review the patient's medical records, conduct an interview if possible, and review all tests given to the patient. The key element of monitoring, according to the ASA, is that "qualified anesthesia personnel shall be continuously present to monitor the patient and provide anesthesia care."[46] This requirement takes in both qualified anesthesiologists and also nurse anesthetists and doctors training in anesthesia, as long as they are under an anesthesiologist's direct supervision.

Postoperative standards include a properly equipped postanesthesia care unit (PACU) to which the patient must be accompanied by a member of the surgical anesthesia team. The person accompanying the patient

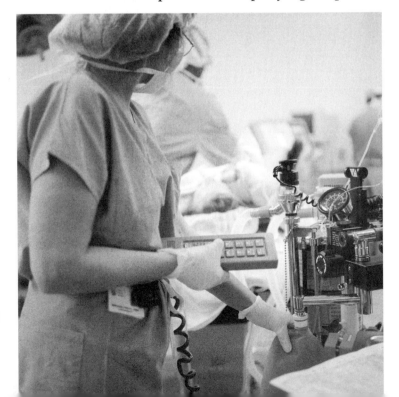

An anesthesiologist monitors an anesthesia machine during an operation.

is required to give an oral report to the PACU nursing staff on the patient's condition and what anesthetics have been administered. The PACU staff may
discharge the patient only when criteria approved by
the hospital's anesthesiology staff have been met.

No Sure Solution

Doctors concede that nothing—safer drugs, better technology, better training of personnel—will completely
eliminate the risks of anesthesia. The basic situation
remains much the same as in 1892, when prominent
Canadian physician William Osler said, "Errors in judg-
ment must occur in the practice of an art which con-
sists largely in balancing probabilities."[47] Anesthesia's
balancing act will only become more difficult as new
technology brings more factors into play.

Another challenge will be the pressure on the medical
profession by hospital administrators to cut costs. Pierce
says, "This is the era of cost-containment, production-
pressure, and bottom-line decision making by corporate
deal-makers. The forces underlying this new era are dri-
ving us to be leaner, faster, and cheaper."[48] He called on
anesthesiologists to stand firm against such pressure.
Anesthesiologists, in the words of Nikolaus Gravenstein
of the University of Florida, must "raise our voices in
support of safety. If we do not, safety will take a back-
seat to economy."[49]

CHAPTER 7

New Directions

The century and a half since the first demonstration of anesthesia in a Boston hospital has seen dramatic improvements in drugs and their delivery, but the basic function of anesthesia—to provide freedom from pain during surgery—has remained. Although this is not likely to change, the role and scope of anesthesiology is taking on added dimensions as medical science looks at both old and new ways of dealing with pain. Indeed, anesthesiologist Nicholas Greene of Yale University advocates substituting the prefix *mete*—to rename the specialty metesthesiology, or "beyond anesthesia."

One of the more recent directions taken by anesthesia —hypnosis—is actually a part of its distant past. Hypnosis, or more specifically mesmerism, was widely practiced in an effort—mostly unsuccessful—to relieve surgical pain prior to the groundbreaking demonstration of ether in 1846, but it quickly fell out of favor thereafter. It never entirely disappeared, however, although its use in the United States and Europe was primarily confined to dentistry.

Hypnosis is achieving new popularity and respectability, not, however, as an anesthetic procedure by itself but as a complement to traditional general and local anesthesia. In particular, doctors have found that hypnosis can greatly boost the effectiveness of anesthetics by reducing the stress and anxiety levels of patients prior to surgery. Patients with reduced stress levels often require lesser amounts of anesthetic drugs. A bonus for patients is that relaxation by hypnosis also can lower blood pressure, resulting in less loss of blood during surgery.

The Iowa Study

Anesthesiologist Sebastian Schulz-Stübner of the University of Iowa conducted a study of forty-eight surgical patients, many of whom had high levels of anxiety about the operations to be performed. "Rather than giving these patients sedating drugs to calm them or make them more relaxed," he says, "we used clinical hypnosis."[50]

Schulz-Stübner found that the vast majority of the patients in the study remembered little or nothing about the surgery afterward. The key to successful use of hypnosis, he says, is to make patients familiar with the procedure well in advance of the operation, something impossible to do for emergency surgeries. Hypnosis was successful in only two of the twelve emergency surgeries included in the study, and those two patients were already familiar with relaxation methods such as yoga.

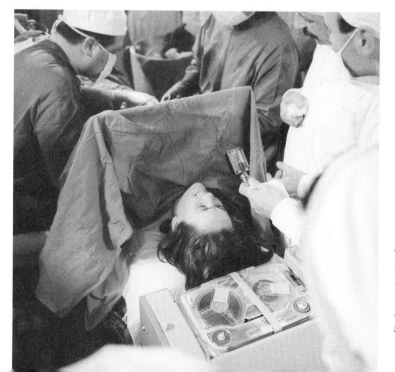

A woman chats with doctors while undergoing an appendectomy under hypnosis in 1961. Hypnosis can reduce the stress and anxiety levels of patients before surgery.

There may be physiological reasons, in addition to psychological factors, why hypnosis can relieve pain. Some doctors think that diminished stress minimizes the production of adrenaline and steroids, thus reducing the body's automatic pain response to trauma. Other researchers, mapping the brain with sophisticated medical imaging devices, have identified one area—the cingulate cortex—that seems to diminish responses to unpleasant stimuli during hypnosis.

Acupuncture

Acupuncture is a second "new" area of anesthesia whose roots extend deep into the past. Used for thousands of years in China, acupuncture is based on the view that pain results from the body being out of harmony because of an imbalance in the flow of a life force known as chi. Acupuncture practitioners insert thin needles into specific points on the body known as meridians. Insertion of the needles supposedly puts the flow of chi into balance.

An instructor demonstrates the art of acupuncture using a model. The insertion of needles at specific points in the body is believed to relieve pain.

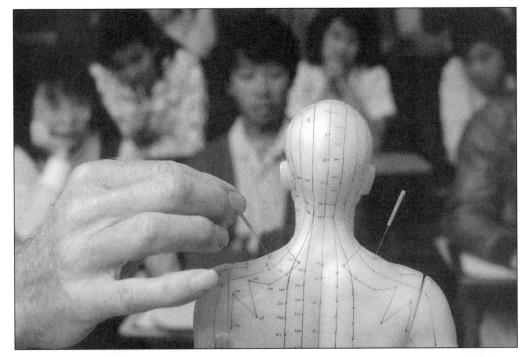

Acupuncture had declined in use, even in China, but it was revived during the Cultural Revolution of the 1960s, when the social chaos resulted in few anesthetics being available to doctors in rural areas. As the United States and China engaged in cultural exchanges during the early 1970s, acupuncture was introduced into the United States. Still, it was practiced mainly in Chinese American communities.

The effectiveness of acupuncture remains the subject of debate. Some practitioners, mostly in Asia, claim that acupuncture can be used in place of general anesthesia for major surgery. Doctors in the United States and Europe, however, normally limit its use to procedures requiring local anesthesia. It seems to have been most successful in dentistry and less successful in surgeries in which muscle relaxation is important. Some doctors have sought to increase its effectiveness by applying electrical current through the metal needles. Even more modern technology has been employed by focusing a laser beam on selected points on the skin.

Acupuncture's Critics

As with hypnosis, acupuncture seems to work best on those patients to whom the procedure has been thoroughly explained. For this reason, some critics of acupuncture claim that its effects are psychological instead of physical. A highly critical 1990 report by the National Council Against Health Fraud (NCAHF) said that acupuncture's positive effects "are probably due to a combination of expectation, suggestion . . . and other psychological mechanisms."[51]

Some researchers suggest, however, that needles inserted near nerves may alter the electromagnetic makeup of nerve cells—much like some anesthetic drugs are thought to do—and thus prevent the flow of pain sensation to the brain. Still others think that the needles, rather than stopping the electrical impulses, increase them, thereby stimulating the release of more painkilling endorphins.

Acupuncture is not a part of the curriculum in Western medical schools, so relatively few doctors in Europe and the Western Hemisphere practice it. As a result, not enough large-scale clinical studies have been conducted to determine its effectiveness. The NCAHF has pointed out what it considers to be flaws in most of the studies claiming positive effects of acupuncture. Indeed, its report says, "the greater the benefit claimed, the worse the experimental design."[52] As more anesthesiologists explore the use of acupuncture, it is possible that more comprehensive clinical studies will be performed and questions about this ancient procedure will be answered.

There is little doubt, however, that acupuncture can relieve pain for some people—not only the pain of surgery but also postoperative pain and even chronic pain. It could be, therefore, that it may prove most valuable in the rapidly expanding field of pain management.

Pain Management

Pain management represents something of a departure for anesthesia, its practitioners, and, indeed, for the practice of medicine. The traditional role of anesthesiology has been to prevent the pain of surgery. The traditional response of doctors to their patients' pain has been to look for, and cure, the cause. The focus on causes, however, leaves doctors unprepared to deal with pain from chronic or terminal conditions or even pain that has no easily isolated cause—pain such as that suffered by patients with cancer or AIDS or those with rheumatoid arthritis or degenerative bone diseases that result in constant joint or back pain.

Pain management involves thinking about anesthesia in an entirely different way—long-term and constant use of anesthetics rather than short-term use to counter the pain of surgery. The challenge becomes not only to stop the pain but also to deal with the side effects, such as irritation to the stomach lining or even physical addiction.

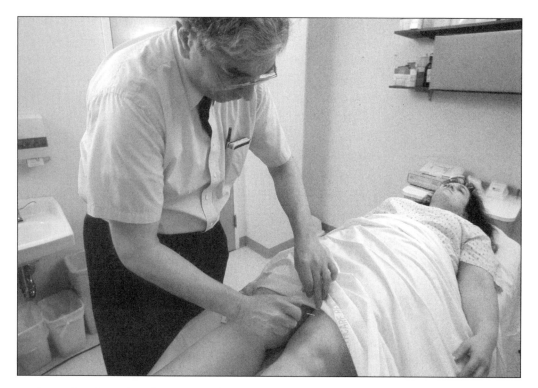

Anesthesia as it relates to pain management involves much more than anesthesiology. The effects of chronic pain—and its treatments—on both the body and mind require contributions from internal medicine, neurology, neurological surgery, orthopedic surgery, and psychiatry. One challenge, therefore, is for practitioners in these various specialties to put aside a tendency to defend their turf in favor of a more collaborative approach. Some anesthesiologists, for example, are concerned that other branches of medicine may dominate the pain management field, attracting a larger share of limited research funds.

A physician applies an acupuncture needle to the leg of a chronic sinusitis patient. Acupuncture has proved to be a valuable tool in the growing field of pain management.

The Importance of Research

Research, in fact, is the lifeblood of the future of anesthesia just as it is for every facet of medicine. Even as anesthesiologists explore new areas of patient care and revisit some of the practices they might once have rejected as superstitious mumbo jumbo, they have by no means neglected their traditional role. Indeed, if they have learned anything, it is that knowledge of new anesthetics, new ways of administering them, and new technologies in patient monitoring will expand at an ever more rapid rate.

Pharmaceutical companies are perhaps setting the fastest pace as they compete to find newer, quicker, and safer anesthetic drugs. Where doctors once had only two choices—ether or chloroform—they now have a vast arsenal of drugs to relieve specific kinds of pain in specific areas of the body. No sooner is a drug discovered, it seems, than it produces numerous offspring. The opioid fentanyl, first used in the 1960s, is about eighty times more powerful than morphine. Subsequent research, however, produced an entire family of fentanyl spin-offs—alfentanil, sufentanil, remifentanil—all used in slightly different ways. There is even carfentanil, so potent—ten thousand times more so than morphine—that it is used almost exclusively

Practice Makes Perfect

In his presentation of the thirty-fourth annual Rovenstine Lecture at the 1995 annual meeting of the American Society of Anesthesiology, Dr. Ellison C. Pierce urged his colleagues to take advantage of technology to increase patient safety by practicing on machines rather than on patients. He called for increased use of simulators to train both student anesthesiologists and veteran practitioners.

In the lecture, found on the Global Anesthesiology Server Network website, Pierce says:

How can human performance be improved? Howard Schwid has provided a key insight in his studies of simulated events such as anaphylaxis and cardiac arrest. Typically, practitioners develop "fixation" errors (i.e. cognitive failure to revise a therapy plan in the face of contradictory evidence). Many investigators and educators now believe that human performance can best be enhanced by the specialized training afforded by realistic simulators. Two commercial models of anesthesia simulators are now available. . . . Use of simulators as training devices, then, is expanding rapidly for teaching basic anesthesia skills, for introducing crisis resource management to individual anesthesiologists and operating room teams, and for investigating the basic foundations and limitations of human performance.

by veterinarians to sedate large animals such as grizzly bears or elephants.

The Perfect Anesthetic

Although there are hundreds of anesthetics that will do something, science has yet to find the single drug that will do everything. In his whimsical article "The Future of Anesthesia," Steven L. Shafer of Stanford University describes the perfect anesthetic: "You turn it on, the patient turns off. You turn it off, the patient turns on."[53]

In his fantasy, written as if he were living in the year 2010, Shafer marvels over the latest drug discoveries. Duzital, for instance, he envisions as "an hypnotic, analgesic, anxiolytic [anxiety reliever], amnestic, muscle relaxant, and aphrodisiac."[54] His crystal ball shows other drugs that combine all the best qualities of today's anesthetics while having none of the disadvantages. His ultimate inhalant, Cyclofurane, even smells like a popular scented home cleanser, and the latest muscle relaxant goes by the name Rockandrolium. The point of Shafer's humor is to show that no one can predict what the anesthetics of the future will be except that those we now consider the best will probably seem primitive by comparison.

The Role of Technology

Such radical developments will be made possible only by the advance of technology. The earliest anesthesia research consisted of pioneers like Faraday, Davy, and Simpson sitting around inhaling fumes from various substances. Investigating the properties of anesthetics today involves powerful computers that can simulate the workings of the human body. A 2001 University of Pittsburgh study on the interaction of halothane with cell membranes, for instance, required 240 hours of processing on a CRAY T3E supercomputer.

Computers, indeed, are likely to play an increasingly important role, not only in research but also in direct patient care. John Oyston of the Scarborough Hospital in Toronto predicts that anesthesia in the future will be delivered not by a mere machine but by an anesthesia information system (AIS).

The AIS will begin, Oyston writes, by recognizing the anesthesiologist's thumbprint and automatically setting its displays to the doctor's individual preference. All information concerning the patient will have been entered and available for display on a monitor screen. The AIS will also have been told who the surgeon will be and thus will know about how long the procedure will last and if the surgeon has any preference of anesthetics.

In addition, the AIS will be a communications center, connected to a telephone, voice mail, the Internet, and other operating rooms within the hospital to make instant videoconferencing possible. Anesthesiologists will be able to view all displays projected on special wireless monitors mounted in eyeglasses, so they will be free to move about the room. Oyston makes the point that, unlike Shafer's whimsical view of the future, all the technology needed for the AIS is now available.

Legal Concerns

One aspect of the AIS that is sure to be controversial because of its potential for exposing doctors to more malpractice lawsuits would be the machine's ability to record all aspects of the anesthesia and the patient's reaction to it. Such a device, similar to the black box recorders on airplanes, would be a valuable tool for improving patient safety. Such databases exist in a few countries, but not in the United States. "We've tried for years," says Ellison C. Pierce, a past chairman of the Anesthesia Patient Safety Foundation, "but because of the legality, the possibility of lawsuits anytime you report anything to anybody, there's no protection. We haven't been able to figure out a way to do it."[55]

Other growing areas of controversy facing anesthesia are where it is administered and by whom. The

Involvement Is Needed

In his online article "The Future of the 'Anesthesia Machine,'" Dr. John Oyston cautions that, if anesthesiologists wish to ensure the best possible technology, they must be directly involved in the design process.

Developments in fast, inexpensive, small, powerful computers, wireless technology, and the Internet are revolutionizing anesthesia in many ways, including better patient monitoring, easier, more accurate record keeping, and improved patient care through the use of expert systems.

However, anesthesiologists must take a leading role in the development and implementation of new technology. If we allow engineers and business executives to develop the tools we use every day, we may find that they fail to incorporate the features we need, include undesirable features, and are inconvenient to use.

If we allow others to decide what features should be incorporated in new operating room technology, we have only ourselves to blame if we find the end product unsatisfying or difficult to use, that it incorporates features that are useless and fails to provide features that would be of advantage to us.

"where" part of the issue deals with the increasing use of anesthesia in physicians' offices rather than in hospitals. Surgical techniques have advanced to the point that many operations can be done in doctors' offices, but although the surgical equipment may be the equal of a hospital's, some professionals are less sure about the facilities for anesthesia. "It's not unusual for the surgery to be going on in an office in which there's no resuscitation equipment, no one trained in resuscitation, in recovery room care," Pierce says. "Since the [Anesthesia Patient Safety] Foundation is not a regulatory organization, all we can do is recommend the states look at this."[56]

Turf Questions

The question of who administers anesthesia involves the American Medical Association (AMA) and the American Society of Anesthesiologists (ASA) on one side and the American Association of Nurse Anesthetists (AANA) on the other. The nurses have sought passage of legislation in several states that would allow them to practice independently of licensed anesthesiologists. The

AMA and the ASA have fought such bills, claiming they would diminish patient safety. The AANA contends that the physicians are only worried that they would receive fewer fees as a result of competition.

At least one person, Jane Fitch of the Baylor College of Medicine in Houston, has been on both sides of the fence. Once a nurse anesthetist and now an anesthesiologist, she says:

> It's in the best interest of patient safety to place nurse anesthetists under the supervision of an anesthesiologist or operating surgeon. After six months as a nurse anesthetist, I became frustrated that I didn't know enough about the patients or the procedures.[57]

Patient Control

Increasingly, however, it is neither the nurse nor the physician who administers anesthesia but rather the patient—at least after the surgery. Patient-controlled anesthesia (PCA) was developed during the 1980s and

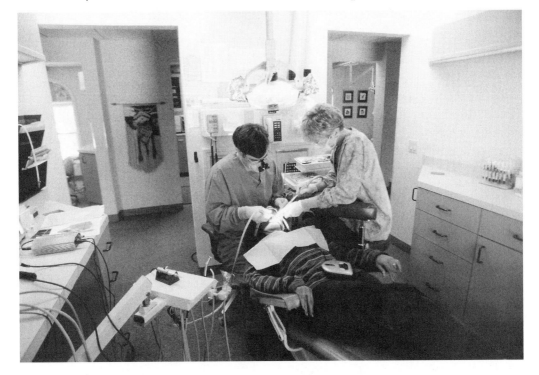

A dentist performs surgery in his office. Anesthesia is frequently administered in physicians' offices lacking resuscitation equipment and trained resuscitation personnel.

Peace Offering or Ploy?

In 2000 the American Society of Anesthesiologists (ASA) formed a committee to design what it called an educational affiliate membership category that would include nurse anesthetists. Instead of making peace in the disagreement between anesthesiologists and nurse anesthetists over the issue of physician control, however, it only fueled the fires of controversy.

The sticking point is that affiliate members would have to agree to the principle that all anesthesia should be under the direct control of a licensed physician. Nurse anesthetists have been trying to get legislation passed at the state level that would allow them to practice independently.

"I think it's just a political play to divide and conquer," said Jan Stewart, then-president of the American Association of Nurse Anesthetists, as quoted in Todd Stein's online article "Struggling for Autonomy."

But Ronald McKenzie, who was president of the ASA, countered, "The ASA is not against nurse anesthetists. We're against unsupervised, independent nurse anesthesia. We don't think it's safe."

The new membership category did little to stop the controversy. The January 2002 newsletter of the ASA reported that it had been successful in convincing the administration of President George W. Bush to postpone implementation of a federal ruling that would have allowed independent practice by nurses and to propose a new rule calling for supervision by physicians.

was in widespread use during the mid-1990s. A container of anesthetic is connected by a thin tube to a site near the surgery or near a nerve that would block pain at the site. The patient, on feeling pain, can push a button, releasing a small dose of the anesthetic. The machines are equipped with safeguards against overdose.

The PCA concept moved outside the hospital during the late 1990s with the development of the pain pump. The pain pump is similar to the in-hospital PCA machine, except that the frequency and size of dosages are controlled by a computer chip. The dosages are programmed to be stronger in the days immediately following the surgery and to gradually diminish and finally cease at about the time the patient has a followup appointment with the surgeon. The safety of pain pumps is debated by surgeons and anesthesiologists and is the subject of many clinical trials.

Horace Wells, William T.G. Morton, and John Warren could scarcely have imagined that what they began in 1846 could result in something like the pain pump. Doctors and researchers today can only guess at what discoveries lie just over the horizon that might at last bring complete freedom from pain. As Steven L. Shafer writes:

> I look into my crystal ball, and I see imagination and dreams. The imagination belongs to scientists and investigators, who extrapolate from what they know today to what they can imagine for tomorrow. The dreams belong to the clinicians, always seeking to provide the best possible care for their patients.[58]

NOTES

Introduction: Now and Then

1. Quoted in Julie M. Fenster, *Ether Day*. New York: HarperCollins, 2001, p. 22.

Chapter 1: Knife and Pain

2. Quoted in René Fülöp-Miller, *Triumph over Pain*. New York: Literary Guild of America, 1938, p. 2.
3. Quoted in Fülöp-Miller, *Triumph over Pain*, p. 6.
4. Quoted in Fenster, *Ether Day*, p. 12.
5. Quoted in Thomas E. Keys, *The History of Surgical Anesthesia*. New York: Dover, 1963, p. 7.
6. Quoted in Fülöp-Miller, *Triumph over Pain*, p. 23.
7. Quoted in G.B. Rushman, N.J.H. Davies, and R.S. Atkinson, *A Short History of Anaesthesia*. Oxford, England: Butterworth-Heinemann, 1996, p. 65.

Chapter 2: First Steps, False Starts

8. Quoted in M.H. Armstrong Davison, *The Evolution of Anesthesia*. Baltimore: Williams & Wilkins, 1965, p. 111.
9. Quoted in Davison, *The Evolution of Anesthesia*, p. 112.
10. Quoted in Fülöp-Miller, *Triumph over Pain*, p. 71.
11. Quoted in Fenster, *Ether Day*, p. 45.
12. Quoted in Fenster, *Ether Day*, p. 35.
13. Quoted in Fenster, *Ether Day*, p. 36.
14. Quoted in Grace Steele Woodward, *The Man Who Conquered Pain*. Boston: Beacon, 1962, p. 38.
15. Quoted in Fülöp-Miller, *Triumph over Pain*, p. 101.

16. Quoted in Fenster, *Ether Day*, p. 39.

Chapter 3: "No Humbug"

17. Quoted in Betty MacQuitty, *Victory over Pain: Morton's Discovery of Anesthesia*. New York: Taplinger, 1971, p. 67.
18. Quoted in Jürgen Thorwald, *The Century of the Surgeon*. New York: Pantheon Books, 1957, p. 98.
19. Quoted in MacQuitty, *Victory over Pain*, p. 42.
20. Quoted in Fenster, *Ether Day*, p. 18.
21. Quoted in Fenster, *Ether Day*, p. 64.
22. Quoted in Robert H. Curtis, *Triumph over Pain: The Story of Anesthesia*. New York: David McKay, 1972, p. 56.
23. Quoted in MacQuitty, *Victory over Pain*, p. 74.
24. Quoted in Thorwald, *The Century of the Surgeon*, pp. 108–109.
25. Quoted in Fülöp-Miller, *Triumph over Pain*, p. 150.
26. Quoted in MacQuitty, *Victory over Pain*, p. 92.
27. Quoted in Woodward, *The Man Who Conquered Pain*, p. 80.

Chapter 4: Chloroform and the Spread of Anesthesia

28. Quoted in Curtis, *Triumph over Pain*, p. 67.
29. Quoted in Fenster, *Ether Day*, p. 168.
30. Quoted in Thorwald, *The Century of the Surgeon*, p. 30.
31. Quoted in Fülöp-Miller, *Triumph over Pain*, p. 334.
32. Quoted in Fülöp-Miller, *Triumph over Pain*, p. 165.
33. Fenster, *Ether Day*, p. 120.
34. Quoted in Fülöp-Miller, *Triumph over Pain*, p. 167.
35. Quoted in Fülöp-Miller, *Triumph over Pain*, p. 168.
36. Quoted in MacQuitty, *Victory over Pain*, p. 93.
37. Quoted in Woodward, *"The Man Who Conquered Pain*, p. 75.
38. Quoted in Keys, *The History of Surgical Anesthesia*, p. 36.
39. Quoted in Keys, *The History of Surgical Anesthesia*, p. 36.

Chapter 5: New Drugs, Deliveries, and Deliverers

40. Quoted in Curtis, *Triumph over Pain*, p. 87.

Chapter 6: Mixed Blessing

41. Quoted in Claudia Kalb, "Taking a New Look at Pain," *Newsweek*, May 19, 2003, p. 45.
42. Ellison C. Pierce, "Forty Years Behind the Mask: Safety Revisited," Anesthesia Patient Safety Foundation. www.gasnet.org.
43. Quoted in Rushman, Davies, and Atkinson, *A Short History of Anaesthesia*, p. 154.
44. Quoted in Pierce, "Forty Years Behind the Mask."
45. Quoted in Pierce, "Forty Years Behind the Mask."
46. American Society of Anesthesiologists, "Standards of the American Society of Anesthesiologists." www.asahq.org.
47. Quoted in American College of Physicians, "Medicine in Quotations Online." www.acponline.org.
48. Pierce, "Forty Years Behind the Mask."
49. Quoted in Pierce, "Forty Years Behind the Mask."

Chapter 7: New Directions

50. Quoted in Jennifer L. Brown, "Physician Studies Hypnosis as Sedation Alternative," University of Iowa news release. www.uiowa.edu.
51. National Council Against Health Fraud, "NCAHF Position Paper on Acupuncture (1990)." www.ncahf.org.
52. National Council Against Health Fraud, "NCAHF Position Paper on Acupuncture (1990)."
53. Steven L. Shafer, "Anesthesia in the Future," *Nouveles Techniques en Anesthésie Générale, JEPU Proceedings*, 1998.
54. Shafer, "Anesthesia in the Future."
55. Pierce, "Forty Years Behind the Mask."
56. Pierce, "Forty Years Behind the Mask."
57. Quoted in Jay Greene, "Anesthesia Turf War Heats Up in Battle over Supervision," *American Medical News*, American Medical Association. www.ama-assn.org.
58. Shafer, "Anesthesia in the Future."

FOR FURTHER READING

Books

Dennis B. Fradin, *We Have Conquered Pain.* New York: M.K. McElderry Books, 1966. A good overview of the discovery of anesthesia for younger readers.

Judith C. Galas, *Anesthetics: Surgery Without Pain.* San Diego: Lucent Books, 1992. A comprehensive treatment of the discovery of anesthesia and subsequent developments.

Irwin Shapiro, *The Gift of Magic Sleep.* New York: Coward, McCann & Geohagen, 1979. This book examines the contributions of Crawford Long, Horace Wells, William Morton, and Charles Jackson, both their discoveries and the subsequent controversies.

Websites

Anesthesia History Files (www.anes.uab.edu/aneshist/ aneshist.htm). A comprehensive list of links to different Internet resources provided by the University of Alabama at Birmingham.

Anesthesia Patient Safety Foundation (www.apsf.org). Interesting and readable articles on anesthesia safety are available from back issues of the foundation's newsletter.

The Deep Blue Book (www.arss.org/book/anestezi. htm). Maintained by the Anesthesiology and Reanimation Specialists Society of Turkey, this interesting site gives not only historical information but also links to articles on pharmacology, safety, techniques, and technology.

Works Consulted

Books

Frank Kells Boland, *The First Anesthetic: The Story of Crawford Long.* Athens: University of Georgia Press, 1950. A very sympathetic story of the man who first discovered anesthesia but did not share the discovery with the world.

Robert H. Curtis, *Triumph over Pain: The Story of Anesthesia.* New York: David McKay, 1972. A history of the early days of anesthesia with particular attention to the use of ether, chloroform, and nitrous oxide.

M.H. Armstrong Davison, *The Evolution of Anesthesia.* Baltimore: Williams & Wilkins, 1965. A comprehensive outline of the history of anesthesia; especially valuable in discussion of events prior to its discovery.

Julie M. Fenster, *Ether Day.* New York: HarperCollins, 2001. A fascinating account not only of the discovery of anesthesia but also of the tragic fates of three of the principal figures in the discovery.

René Fülöp-Miller, *Triumph over Pain.* New York: Literary Guild of America, 1938. A dated but highly detailed and readable account of the discovery of anesthesia and the subsequent fortunes of the discoverers.

Thomas E. Keys, *The History of Surgical Anesthesia.* New York: Dover, 1963. A very thorough examination of the progress made in the field of anesthesia during the century after its discovery.

Betty MacQuitty, *Victory over Pain: Morton's Discovery of*

Anesthesia. New York: Taplinger, 1971. A very sympathetic treatment of the life of William T.G. Morton. It makes light of some of Morton's character flaws and minimizes the contributions of Horace Wells and others.

G.B. Rushman, N.J.H. Davies, and R.S. Atkinson, *A Short History of Anaesthesia.* Oxford, England: Butterworth-Heinemann, 1996. A highly detailed but often highly technical and very dry account of anesthesia from 1846 to the present.

Philip Smith, *Arrows of Mercy.* Garden City, NY: Doubleday, 1969. A fascinating story of how a deadly poison from the jungles of South America was transformed into an invaluable surgical tool.

Jürgen Thorwald, *The Century of the Surgeon.* New York: Pantheon Books, 1957. A highly entertaining and imaginatively written account of the development of surgery thanks to the discoveries of anesthesia, antiseptics, and other medical innovations.

Grace Steele Woodward, *The Man Who Conquered Pain.* Boston: Beacon, 1962. A biography of William T.G. Morton that, like the one by MacQuitty, gives him most of the credit for the discovery of anesthesia at the expense of others.

Periodicals

Robert A. Caplan, "Liability Arising from Anesthesia Gas Delivery Equipment," *ASA Newsletter,* June 1998.

Frederick W. Cheney, "Perioperative Ulnar Nerve Injury—a Continuing Medical and Liability Problem," *ASA Newsletter,* June 1998.

Karen B. Domino, "Closed Malpractice Claims for Airway Trauma During Anesthesia," *ASA Newsletter,* June 1998.

Claudia Kalb, "Taking a New Look at Pain," *Newsweek,* May 19, 2003.

Mark J. Lema, "1913–2013," *ASA Newsletter,* January 2000.

Mary Brophy Marcus, "How Does Anesthesia Work?" *U.S. News & World Report,* August 18, 1997.

Karen L. Posner, "Closed Claims Project Shows Safety Evolution," *ASA Newsletter*, Fall 2001.

Steven L. Shafer, "Anesthesia in the Future," *Nouveles Techniques en Anesthésie Générale, JEPU Proceedings*, 1998.

Patrick P. Sims, "Anesthesiology, Anesthesiologist, Anesthetics, and Anesthetist: The Emerging Professionalism of a Medical Society," *ASA Newsletter*, September 2000.

Internet Sources

American Association of Nurse Anesthetists, "Nurse Anesthetists at a Glance." www.aana.com.

American College of Physicians, "Medicine in Quotations Online." www.acponline.org.

American Society of Anesthesiologists, "History." www.asahq.org.

———, "Standards of the American Society of Anesthesiologists." www.asahq.org.

Anesthesiology Info, "How Does Anesthesia Work?" January 14, 2001. www.anesthesiologyinfo.com.

Applesforhealth.com, "Redheads Require More Anesthesia," October 25, 2002. www.applesforhealth.com.

Bill Bornstein, "Medical Mistakes: Human Error or System Failure?" *Momentum*, Fall 2000. www.emory.edu.

Jennifer L. Brown, "Physician Studies Hypnosis as Sedation Alternative," University of Iowa news release. www.uiowa.edu.

Capitol Anesthesiology Association, "Are There Risks to Having Anesthesia?" 2003. www.capanes.com.

Jeffrey B. Cooper, "Critical Incidents, Anesthesia Safety and Record Keeping," *Anesthesia Patient Safety Foundation Newsletter*, Winter 2000. www.apsf.org.

Focusing on Words, "Facts About Anesthesia's Past." www.wordfocus.com.

Jay Greene, "Anesthesia Turf War Heats Up in Battle over Supervision," *American Medical News*, American Medical Association. www.ama-assn.org.

Christopher Guadoagnino, "Improving Anesthesia Safety," *Physician's News Digest.* www.physicians news.com.

Institute for the Study of Healthcare Organizations, "Anesthesia and Surgery," September 2000. www.institute-shot.com.

National Council Against Health Fraud, "NCAHF Position Paper on Acupuncture (1990)." www.ncahf.org.

New York State Society of Anesthesiologists, "The 1900s and Organized Anesthesia." www.nyssa-pga.org.

John Oyston, "The Future of the 'Anesthesia Machine.'" www.oyston.com.

Linus Pauling, "A Molecular Theory of General Anesthesia," Linus Pauling Papers, Profiles in Science, National Library of Medicine. www.nlm.nih.gov.

Lina Pesu, "Illustrating the Modern Anesthesia Concept," Clinical Window. www.clinicalwindow.com.

Ellison C. Pierce, "Forty Years Behind the Mask: Safety Revisited," Anesthesia Patient Safety Foundation. www.gasnet.org.

Projects in Scientific Computing, University of Pittsburg, "The Road to La-La Land." www.psc.edu/science.

Don R. Revis, "Local Anesthetics," Emedicine. www.emedicine.com.

Todd Stein, "Struggling for Autonomy," February 17, 2000. www.nurseweek.com.

Michel Struys, "Introduction to the Concept of General Anesthesia," Clinical Window. www.clinicalwindow.com.

Surgery Door Pain Centre, "What Is Pain?" July 25, 2000. www.surgerydoor.co.uk.

J.M. Tuckley, "The Pharmacology of Local Anesthetic Agents," World Federation of Societies of Anesthesi-ologists. www.nda.ox.ac.us/wfsa.

Walter Reed Army Medical Center, "Basic Anesthetic Monitoring." www.wramc.amedd.army.mil.

Jay Z. Yeh, "Pharmacology of General Anesthesia," Neurology Department, Feinberg School of Medicine, Northwestern University. www.neuro.nwu.edu.

INDEX

PICTURE CREDITS

About the Author

William W. Lace is a native of Fort Worth, Texas. He holds a bachelor's degree from Texas Christian University, a master's degree from East Texas State University, and a doctorate from the University of North Texas. After writing for newspapers in Baytown, Texas, and Fort Worth, he joined the University of Texas at Arlington, eventually becoming director of the News Service. He is now executive assistant to the chancellor at Tarrant County College in Fort Worth. He has written more than twenty books for Lucent, one of which—*The Death Camps* in the Holocaust Library series—was selected by the New York Public Library for its 1999 Recommended Teenage Reading List. He and his wife Laura, a retired school librarian, live in Arlington, Texas, and have two grown children.